Freedom of Speech,
Second Edition

Freedom of Speech,
Second Edition

**Alan Allport &
Jennifer Horner**

Series Editor
Alan Marzilli, M.A., J.D.

CHELSEA HOUSE
An Infobase Learning Company

Freedom of Speech, Second Edition

Copyright © 2011 by Infobase Learning

All rights reserved. No part of this book may be reproduced or utilized in any form
or by any means, electronic or mechanical, including photocopying, recording, or by
any information storage or retrieval systems, without permission in writing from the
publisher. For information, contact:

Chelsea House
An imprint of Infobase Learning
132 West 31st Street
New York, NY 10001

Library of Congress Cataloging-in-Publication Data
Allport, Alan, 1970–
Freedom of speech / by Alan Allport and Jennifer Horner.— 2nd ed.
p. cm. — (Point-counterpoint)
Includes bibliographical references and index.
ISBN 978-1-60413-759-0 (hardcover)
1. Freedom of speech—United States—Juvenile literature. I. Horner, Jennifer.
II. Title. III. Series.

KF4772.A95 2011
342.7308'53—dc22

2010026484

Chelsea House books are available at special discounts when purchased in bulk
quantities for businesses, associations, institutions, or sales promotions. Please call
our Special Sales Department in New York at (212) 967-8800 or (800) 322-8755.

You can find Chelsea House on the World Wide Web at http://www.chelseahouse.com.

Text design by Keith Trego
Cover design by Alicia Post
Composition by EJB Publishing Services
Cover printed by Yurchak Printing, Landisville, Pa.
Book printed and bound by Yurchak Printing, Landisville, Pa.
Date printed: April 2011
Printed in the United States of America

10 9 8 7 6 5 4 3 2 1

This book is printed on acid-free paper.

All links and Web addresses were checked and verified to be correct at the time of
publication. Because of the dynamic nature of the Web, some addresses and links
may have changed since publication and may no longer be valid.

Alan Marzilli, M.A., J.D.
Birmingham, Alabama

The POINT/COUNTERPOINT series offers the reader a greater understanding of some of the most controversial issues in contemporary American society—issues such as capital punishment, immigration, gay rights, and gun control. We have looked for the most contemporary issues and have included topics—such as the controversies surrounding "blogging"—that we could not have imagined when the series began.

In each volume, the author has selected an issue of particular importance and set out some of the key arguments on both sides of the issue. Why study both sides of the debate? Maybe you have yet to make up your mind on an issue, and the arguments presented in the book will help you to form an opinion. More likely, however, you will already have an opinion on many of the issues covered by the series. There is always the chance that you will change your opinion after reading the arguments for the other side. But even if you are firmly committed to an issue—for example, school prayer or animal rights—reading both sides of the argument will help you to become a more effective advocate for your cause. By gaining an understanding of opposing arguments, you can develop answers to those arguments.

Perhaps more importantly, listening to the other side sometimes helps you see your opponent's arguments in a more human way. For example, Sister Helen Prejean, one of the nation's most visible opponents of capital punishment, has been deeply affected by her interactions with the families of murder victims. By seeing the families' grief and pain, she understands much better why people support the death penalty, and she is able to carry out her advocacy with a greater sensitivity to the needs and beliefs of death penalty supporters.

The books in the series include numerous features that help the reader to gain a greater understanding of the issues. Real-life examples illustrate the human side of the issues. Each chapter also includes excerpts from relevant laws, court cases, and other material, which provide a better foundation for understanding the arguments. The volumes contain citations to relevant sources of law and information, and an appendix guides the reader through the basics of legal research, both on the Internet and in the library. Today, through free Web sites, it is easy to access legal documents, and these books might give you ideas for your own research.

Studying the issues covered by the POINT/COUNTERPOINT series is more than an academic activity. The issues described in the books affect all of us as citizens. They are the issues that today's leaders debate and tomorrow's leaders will decide. While all of the issues covered in the POINT/COUNTERPOINT series are controversial today, and will remain so for the foreseeable future, it is entirely possible that the reader might one day play a central role in resolving the debate. Today it might seem that some debates—such as capital punishment and abortion—will never be resolved.

However, our nation's history is full of debates that seemed as though they never would be resolved, and many of the issues are now well settled—at least on the surface. In the nineteenth century, abolitionists met with widespread resistance to their efforts to end slavery. Ultimately, the controversy threatened the union, leading to the Civil War between the northern and southern states. Today, while a public debate over the merits of slavery would be unthinkable, racism persists in many aspects of society.

Similarly, today nobody questions women's right to vote. Yet at the beginning of the twentieth century, suffragists fought public battles for women's voting rights, and it was not until the passage of the Nineteenth Amendment in 1920 that the legal right of women to vote was established nationwide.

What makes an issue controversial? Often, controversies arise when most people agree that there is a problem but disagree about the best way to solve it. There is little argument that poverty is a major problem in the United States, especially in inner cities and rural areas. Yet, people disagree vehemently about the best way to address the problem. To some, the answer is social programs, such as welfare, food stamps, and public housing. However, many argue that such subsidies encourage dependence on government benefits while unfairly penalizing those who work and pay taxes, and that the real solution is to require people to support themselves.

American society is in a constant state of change, and sometimes modern practices clash with what many consider to be "traditional values," which are often rooted in conservative political views or religious beliefs. Many blame high crime rates, and problems such as poverty, illiteracy, and drug use on the breakdown of the traditional family structure of a married mother and father raising their children. Since the "sexual revolution" of the 1960s and 1970s, sparked in part by the widespread availability of the birth control pill, marriage rates have declined, and the number of children born outside of marriage has increased. The sexual revolution led to controversies over birth control, sex education, and other issues, most prominently abortion. Similarly, the gay rights movement has been challenged as a threat to traditional values. While many gay men and lesbians want to have the same right to marry and raise families as heterosexuals, many politicians and others have challenged gay marriage and adoption as a threat to American society.

Sometimes, new technology raises issues that we have never faced before, and society disagrees about the best solution. Are people free to swap music online, or does this violate the copyright laws that protect songwriters' and musicians' ownership of the music that they create? Should scientists use "genetic engineering" to create new crops that are resistant to disease and pests and produce more food, or is it too risky to use a laboratory to create plants that nature never intended? Modern medicine has continued to increase the average lifespan—which is now 77 years, up from under 50 years at the beginning of the twentieth century—but many people are now choosing to die in comfort rather than living with painful ailments in their later years. For doctors, this presents an ethical dilemma: should they allow their patients to die? Should they assist patients in ending their own lives painlessly?

Perhaps the most controversial issues are those that implicate a Constitutional right. The Bill of Rights—the first 10 Amendments to the U.S. Constitution—spells out some of the most fundamental rights that distinguish our democracy from other nations with fewer freedoms. However, the sparsely worded document is open to interpretation, with each side saying that the Constitution is on their side. The Bill of Rights was meant to protect individual liberties; however, the needs of some individuals clash with society's needs. Thus, the Constitution often serves as a battleground between individuals and government officials seeking to protect society in some way. The First Amendment's guarantee of "freedom of speech" leads to some very difficult questions. Some forms of expression—such as burning an American flag—lead to public outrage, but are protected by the First Amendment. Other types of expression that most people find objectionable—such as child pornography—are not protected by the Constitution. The question is not only where to draw the line, but whether drawing lines around constitutional rights threatens our liberty.

The Bill of Rights raises many other questions about individual rights and societal "good." Is a prayer before a high school football game an "establishment of religion" prohibited by the First Amendment? Does the Second Amendment's promise of "the right to bear arms" include concealed handguns? Does stopping and frisking someone standing on a known drug corner constitute "unreasonable search and seizure" in violation of the Fourth Amendment? Although the U.S. Supreme Court has the ultimate authority in interpreting the U.S. Constitution, its answers do not always satisfy the public. When a group of nine people—sometimes by a five-to-four vote—makes a decision that affects hundreds of millions of others, public outcry can be expected. For example, the Supreme Court's 1973 ruling in *Roe v. Wade* that abortion is protected by the Constitution did little to quell the debate over abortion.

Whatever the root of the controversy, the books in the POINT/COUNTERPOINT series seek to explain to the reader the origins of the debate, the current state of the law, and the arguments on either side of the debate. Our hope in creating this series is that readers will be better informed about the issues facing not only our politicians, but all of our nation's citizens, and become more actively involved in resolving these debates, as voters, concerned citizens, journalists, or maybe even elected officials.

This newly revised volume examines one of America's fundamental freedoms. The First Amendment of the U.S. Constitution declares that "Congress shall make no law . . . abridging the freedom of speech, or of the press." Although private citizens and the press seem to be entitled to unfettered freedom of expression under the Constitution, the issue is by no means so simple. Some questions raised in the first edition of this volume—such as cross burning, Internet pornography, and the funding of political advertisements—have subsequently been addressed in landmark court cases. New questions always arise, however, with anti-Muslim sentiment developing as a result of the 9/11 terrorist attacks, new forms of Internet communication, and the increasing interplay of American businesses and foreign laws. This volume examines both new and lingering questions about the boundaries of freedom of expression.

Free Speech and the First Amendment

One weekend in February 2000, Nick Emmett, a college-bound senior at a high school near Seattle, Washington, decided to create a lighthearted "unofficial" Web site for the school on his home computer. Prompted by an assignment in a recent writing class, he invented and posted a mock obituary to one of his school friends. The idea caught on, and as other students heard about the site, they asked Nick to write their mock obituaries also. The number of visitors to the site kept increasing, and so Nick added a way for students to vote for the next "death notice." For the first couple of days, everyone praised Nick's site—even some of his teachers, who were impressed by his creativity and could see that it was meant in good fun.

Then a local TV news station did a report about the Web site that put a very sinister spin on the obituaries, implying that Nick was creating some kind of "hit list." Less than a year had passed since the terrible events at Columbine High School in Colorado, in which two students murdered 13 people in a shooting rampage, and fears about student violence were still very fresh in communities throughout America. Nick, who was horrified at the misrepresentation of his Web site on the TV show, decided to remove it from the Internet immediately. Two days later, however, school authorities gave him a week's suspension. Nick and his parents believed that the punishment was unfair, and so they decided to take the matter to federal court. The judge in the case quickly decided that Nick's First Amendment right to freedom of speech had been violated and told the school to end the suspension right away. In the final settlement, the school district removed the punishment from Nick's permanent record and agreed to pay his legal fees. Afterward, Nick said that he was sorry his Web site had caused so much trouble, but he nonetheless believed that "it was good to prove students' rights to free speech."[1]

In the years since Nick posted his spoof Web site, the means for virtual communication have grown exponentially. High school students have been gossiping about their friends and teachers for as long as anyone can remember, but now students can publish their opinions across the globe. Not all of the uses of the Internet are as innocuous as Nick Emmett's. Some student free-speech cases have centered on highly offensive personal attacks on classmates and teachers. Many of these have resulted in suspensions and lawsuits. In one case, a Florida high school student was suspended for creating a Facebook page criticizing her English teacher and inviting other students to contribute negative comments. A court later ruled that the page was protected speech under the First Amendment. But free-speech law does not protect specific threats, as a group of students discovered when a California appeals court ruled that their comments on a classmate's personal Web site constituted hate speech and defamation. Other instances of "cyber-harassment" have not been as clearly resolved. In 2006, a woman harassed her daughter's 13-year-old classmate by posing as a teenage boy on the social networking site MySpace. The initially friendly relationship turned psychologically abusive, and after receiving a barrage of cruel messages from her fictional "friend," the young girl committed suicide. The woman behind the messages was eventually acquitted of federal charges of computer fraud. Clearly, communication in the digital age has brought a new dimension to the already complicated question of free speech in a free society. What is the right balance between fair expression and the rights of the community? What can and cannot be said?

The First Amendment

At the center of all of these issues is the First Amendment to the Constitution of the United States. One of the original 10 amendments (known collectively as the Bill of Rights, which were ratified in 1791), the First Amendment consists of a single sentence:

> Congress shall make no law respecting an establishment of religion, or prohibiting the free exercise thereof; or abridging the freedom of speech, or of the press; or the right of the people peaceably to assemble, and to petition the government for a redress of grievances.

Probably no other sentence in American history has aroused such passions and opened up so many possibilities as the First Amendment. It is also one of the hardest-working clauses in the whole Constitution, because it entrenches no less than five key rights in a row: freedom from government involvement in religion (sometimes known as the "separation of church and state"); freedom of worship; freedom of speech; freedom of the press (the right to publish without government censorship); and the freedom to assemble to discuss and protest about the issues of the day. The first two rights concerning religion are very much in the news—for example, with the 2010 federal court decision that the "under God" portion of the Pledge of

Allegiance is constitutional—but while these are both undoubtedly First Amendment rights, they are somewhat different from other issues concerning free speech.

What the free-speech protections of the First Amendment say, in essence, is that the U.S. government cannot pass laws that interfere with the rights of American citizens to express their opinions about public or private matters. Originally this applied only to federal authorities; state and local governments were included later. The First Amendment also covers public institutions like schools and colleges.

The First Amendment does not mean that Americans are free to say absolutely anything they like whenever and wherever they like: The government is allowed some discretionary powers in the public interest. It does mean, though, that Americans enjoy an unusually large amount of freedom when it comes to speaking their minds. The United States is not unique in having constitutionally protected free speech, but the principle is more broadly interpreted here than in most other countries, even other democratic nations. For example, although there is a long tradition of respecting free speech in the United Kingdom, the British do not have an absolute right to it in law. Similarly, there are restrictions on certain types of free expression in France and Germany that would be ruled unconstitutional in the United States.

Because the First Amendment is a constitutional protection, it carries the ultimate authority of the U.S. Supreme Court. If Americans feel that the authorities have infringed on their right to free speech, they can petition the judiciary to overturn the decision. In most cases a lower federal court reviews the case, although either side, if unsuccessful, can try to appeal the decision to a higher court. If a definitive interpretation of the law is required, it is possible that the Supreme Court itself will agree to hear the case. The Supreme Court's decision is regarded as the final word on the subject, and the precedent it sets may have an important influence on First Amendment rights for years or even generations to come. Only a later Supreme Court decision can overturn a prior one.

Although it was not part of the original document and was only added a few years later, the First Amendment has been described as the keystone of the whole Constitution. This is because the other rights enshrined in that document can only be properly protected through free expression; tyranny can arise only if the people are powerless to speak against it. The Founding

THE LETTER OF THE LAW

Sedition Act (Approved July 14, 1798)

Even with the First Amendment, the government at times has tried to place restrictions on freedom of speech. The Sedition Act of 1798 was an early attempt to set such limits. The act was heavily criticized, but it expired automatically after a few years and was never challenged in the Supreme Court. In part, it read:

[Be it enacted that] if any person shall write, print, utter, or publish, or shall cause or procure to be written, printed, uttered, or published, or shall knowingly and willingly assist or aid in writing, printing, uttering, or publishing any false, scandalous and malicious writing or writings against the government of the United States, or either House of the Congress of the United States, or the President of the United States, with intent to defame the said government, or either House of the said Congress, or the said President, or to bring them, or either of them, into contempt or disrepute, or to excite against them, or either or any of them, the hatred of the good people of the United States, or to stir up sedition within the United States; or to excite any unlawful combinations therein, for opposing or resisting any law of the United States, or any act of the President of the United States, done in pursuance of any such law, or of the powers in him vested by the Constitution of the United States, or to resist, oppose, or defeat any such law or act, or to aid, encourage or abet any hostile designs of any foreign nation against the United States, their people or government, then such person, being thereof convicted before any court of the United States having jurisdiction thereof, shall be punished by a fine not exceeding two thousand dollars, and by imprisonment not exceeding two years.

Fathers believed that the free exchange of opinions was the best guarantee of a healthy and vigorous democracy.

Defining "Speech"

However the founders themselves personally defined speech, the range of modern free-speech protection has extended far beyond the mere spoken or printed word. Speech is now considered to include a whole range of language, gestures, and behaviors; any instance of such expression, linguistic or not, is referred to as a "speech act." One of the more controversial examples is the deliberate burning of the U.S. flag: Although this is obviously not a spoken action, the courts have nonetheless decided that it counts as speech for the purposes of the First Amendment and it is consequently protected. The key factor is that it is an action that communicates an idea. The purpose of the First Amendment was to bolster communication within society, and so if an act is judged to be some kind of medium of information or opinion, it is defined as speech. In recent years the Supreme Court has taken an increasingly broad view of this idea, designating all kinds of behavior as legitimate forms of communication. Although the main focus of the First Amendment has traditionally been on political information and opinion, protected speech does not necessarily have to be overtly political: Even commercial information, like advertising, has some protection under the First Amendment, though to a lesser extent than other forms of speech.

One type of speech that is specifically mentioned in the Constitution is the freedom of the press. The Founding Fathers believed that books and newspapers had an important role to play in the maintenance of a civic democracy, as well as unique responsibilities. Today television, film, radio, and the Internet have joined the traditional forms of the press to create our modern mass media, whose great powers and duties will be explored here in more detail.

Unpopular Speech

The First Amendment was not designed to protect someone's right to say that the sky is blue, because that kind of speech does not need protection. By definition, facts that are uncontroversial are not going to be suppressed by the government, or indeed anyone else, for why would they want to suppress them? The heart of free-speech protection is to defend unpopular ideas, opinions, or information, speech that other people may want forbidden or kept silent. The most important tests of the First Amendment arise at its wilder margins, when it is protecting speech that is very controversial or that challenges standard preconceptions and beliefs.

This is not to suggest that unpopular speech is necessarily worthy. Many ideas are unpopular because they are unpleasant, misleading, bizarre, or simply insane. Very few Americans would agree with the kind of "hate speech" propagated by racist fringe groups; the vast majority would prefer to see these ideas disappear for good. But is the best way to tackle hate speech to tolerate it or to ban it? The topic remains hotly debated and has become even more urgent with the mass publication possibilities of the Internet. The traditional answer given by supporters of the First Amendment is that it is not the government's place to decide which beliefs are good and which are evil. Instead, the "marketplace of ideas" should be the proper forum for this type of decision. Just as in the commercial marketplace, valuable goods and services rise in demand while shoddy ones are passed by, so in the abstract world of argument, worthy ideas will become accepted and bad ones ignored. This sometimes means tolerating opinions that are obnoxious or hateful, but free-speech advocates trust in the common sense of the people to choose only virtuous ideas in the long term. While the marketplace of ideas, as Thomas Jefferson once wrote to James Madison, is "alloyed with some inconveniences," its good "vastly outweighs the evil."[2] This, at least, is the theory—but it is still the subject of great debate.

THOMAS JEFFERSON.

One of the great minds of the American Revolution, Thomas Jefferson was the principal author of the Declaration of Independence (1776) and the third president of the United States (1801–1809). Jefferson believed that tolerating hateful opinions was necessary in order to maintain free speech.

While unpopular opinions are often rightly unpopular, it is important to keep in mind that some ideas that are now commonplace were once considered bizarre or dangerous. In the early to mid-1800s, antislavery campaigners, or abolitionists, were often harassed for their "extreme" views on emancipation and the rights of all people, black and white. Pioneering Victorian feminists who advocated votes for women were depicted as hysterical zealots. Trade unionists faced imprisonment for supporting labor rights. Perhaps current ideas of what are and what are not "normal" beliefs will be considered absurd in years to come. In past years, the Supreme Court has extended First Amendment protection to categories of expression that many Americans find appalling. For example, the brutal "blood sport" of dogfighting is illegal in the United States. In 2010, however, the Supreme Court affirmed the right to sell videos of dogfights, because the law under which a vendor had been convicted was overly broad in its definition of "animal cruelty." The Court argued that, if the law was upheld, it would also ban depictions of legal activities such as hunting and fishing.[3] It is not always easy to tell which ideas will be accepted into the mainstream and which will be ultimately forgotten or rejected, and this is another reason free-speech supporters believe the First Amendment should protect as much expression as possible.

Limitations on Speech

There is no absolute right in America to say anything at all, at any time, about anything. Even the most die-hard advocates of free speech accept that there must be some practical restrictions in the interests of public safety and to protect other rights. There is no right to march into someone else's house uninvited to begin a political oration; here, the law says that the householder's right to privacy comes first. Nor can someone publish confidential information about troop movements in a newspaper during wartime; national security has to be respected and guaranteed, too. As Supreme Court Justice Oliver Wendell Holmes famously put it,

"The most stringent protection of free speech would not protect a man in falsely shouting 'fire' in a theater."[4] The restrictions that the government can put on speech, however, are carefully defined and subject to constant review to prevent abuse.

Free-speech issues are usually divided into two categories: content; and time, place, and manner. The first is concerned with what you can say and the second with when, where, and how you can say it. Restrictions on speech content are very limited. The traditional restriction in the first half of the twentieth century—again, the inspiration of Oliver Wendell Holmes—came as the result of a 1919 Supreme Court case, *Schenck v. United States*, in which an agitator against American involvement in World War I (1914–1918) was prosecuted for distributing materials opposing the draft. Although the justices found against Schenck, the precedent was established that the government could ban speech only if there was a "clear and present danger"[5] of its producing harm to the public. Later, this notion was clarified in what is called "the Brandenburg standard" after the legal case in which it was first used, *Brandenburg v. Ohio* (1969). Clarence Brandenburg was a Ku Klux Klan leader who was prosecuted under a state ordinance outlawing speech that advocated lawless behavior. The Supreme Court threw out his conviction, and as a result of its decision, speech

FROM THE BENCH

Cohen v. California, 403 U.S. 15 (1971)

To many, the immediate consequence of [the freedom of speech] may often appear to be only verbal tumult, discord, and even offensive utterance. These are, however, within established limits, in truth necessary side effects of the broader enduring values which the process of open debate permits us to achieve. That the air may at times seem filled with verbal cacophony is, in this sense, not a sign of weakness but of strength.

can only be suppressed on the grounds of public safety if it is intended, and likely, to produce "imminent lawless action."[6] In other words, vague threats (such as a general speech by a person like Brandenburg or a group that advocates revolution, like the Communist Party) are not enough; the government can only take action in cases in which there is an immediate, demonstrable risk of violence or illegality. There are other content restrictions on the grounds of obscenity and criminal libel, too.

Time, place, and manner restrictions are easier to enforce because they do not totally prevent the communication of ideas; they only limit them in certain contexts. So, for example, city authorities are allowed to require permits in advance for political rallies, on the grounds that they have a responsibility to maintain public order, the smooth flow of traffic, noise control, etc. There are, however, conditions that the authorities have to abide by: The city government cannot hand out its permits in a partisan way, for instance, allowing some groups to protest and forbidding others to do the same. Whenever the state interferes in free speech, it must do so with an even hand, not favoring any one side in an argument.

Also, the courts generally frown on suppressing speech before it is expressed, rather than afterward: Such a restriction is called "prior restraint." Like many American legal principles, the importance—or rather infamy—of prior restraint comes through the heritage of British common law. In 1694, the British Parliament refused to renew an old licensing system for books and periodicals originally created by King Henry VIII, arguing that it was a form of unjust political censorship. The United States inherited this belief that licensing and other types of prior restraint were contrary to the spirit of the Bill of Rights because they involved a severe limitation on free expression. Writers, so the argument went, should be judged based on what they have written, not on what they might write in the future. Although this sense that prior restraint was unconstitutional lingered throughout early American history, it was not until 1931 that the

Supreme Court, in *Near v. Minnesota*, formally confirmed that laws practicing prior restraint should usually be struck down.[7]

Summary

As these examples show, the First Amendment often clashes with other important privileges and responsibilities. In specific cases, it is the job of the courts to decide which one has the highest priority in the best interests of society. Because free speech is such an important right, its restriction is never considered lightly, and the government is permitted to act against it only under genuinely compelling circumstances. Free speech is a constantly negotiated right, one that has its costs as well as its benefits.

Some Ideas Are Dangerous Enough to Merit Restriction

In October 1976, the director of parks and recreation for the small Chicago suburb of Skokie received a request from a group calling itself the National Socialist Party of America to stage a march in the Illinois town. The organization, which advocated the clearly racist policies of Adolf Hitler's Nazi Germany, had not chosen Skokie at random. The town had a large Jewish population, and some residents were survivors of the Nazi concentration camps of World War II (1939–1945). The intention of the marchers was clearly provocative, especially as they planned to wear Nazi-style uniforms and carry swastikas and other symbols of the Third Reich. The Skokie Parks District's board of governors refused the request, and in addition filed an injunction in Illinois' Cook County district court to prevent the Nazis from marching in their town. This was the beginning of the Skokie controversy—one of the most divisive and emotional cases in First Amendment history and also an important bench-mark in the debate over the right to express "hate speech."

The Skokie affair was a complicated, long-running story involving many lawsuits and countersuits in state and federal courts, but in essence what happened was this: The Nazi group asked the Illinois courts to stay, or put on hold, the injunction against it until the group could mount a full appeal. This was refused. Having failed at the state level, the Nazis took their request to the U.S. Supreme Court, where, to the surprise of many, they won. In a narrow five-to-four decision, the Supreme Court forced Illinois to stay its injunction pending appeal.[1] Around the same time, the Skokie town council drew up a set of ordinances banning the wearing of military-style uniforms in political demonstrations and prohibiting the distribution of material that incited hatred against certain racial or religious groups. The Nazis went to court to overturn these ordinances on First Amendment grounds. In February 1978, the federal district court in Illinois ruled that they were indeed unconstitu-tional. Skokie's case effectively collapsed that October when the Supreme Court refused to hear the town's appeal.[2] In fact, no Nazi ever did march in Skokie—the group ultimately canceled its rally, claiming that its "moral victory" was success enough—but the Supreme Court's 1978 decision had repercussions far beyond the Chicago suburbs.

Hate speech is also hate crime.

A 2009 report by the Federal Bureau of Investigation (FBI) detailed more than 8,000 cases of "hate crimes"—offenses against people or property that were motivated by a hatred of another's race, religion, sexual orientation, national origin, or disability.[3] There is a growing debate within the United States about hate-crime legislation and whether criminal behavior involving hate should receive extra punishment in the courts. Hate crimes and hate speech must not be confused, however, for there is an important distinction in law: Hate crimes are

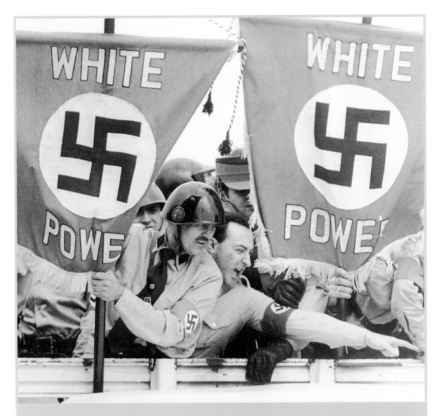

Frank Collin, national director of the National Socialist (Nazi) Party of America, points a finger and shouts at anti-Nazi crowds that lined a parade route through south St. Louis, on March 11, 1978. The crowd jeered and hurled snowballs as the Nazis rode by on a flatbed truck. Collin had called the parade a prelude to a planned Nazi march through predominantly Jewish neighborhoods in Skokie, Illinois.

acts—such as robbery, assault, or murder—that would clearly be illegal and punishable no matter their motivation. There is no question of hate crimes being protected by the Constitution: Nobody in America has a right to harm another person. Nor is active discrimination or harassment in the workplace based on race, sex, religion, etc. legal. But hate speech—the dissemination of hateful ideas and opinions, without acting on them—is trickier. The expression of political viewpoints lies at the heart of the First Amendment, and there is a much less clear-cut justification for prohibiting or punishing such speech. Cases like the 1978 Skokie decision have established the precedent that—as long as it remains speech and not action—hate in America is, effectively, legal and protected.

But why? Traditionally, defenders of free expression have fallen back on an appeal to the marketplace of ideas—or, as English author Evelyn Beatrice Hall once paraphrased French philosopher Voltaire, "I disapprove of what you say, but I will defend to the death your right to say it."[4] After all, speech is not action—so the old claim goes. Yet this division between thought and deed, while it makes for a nice philosophical distinction, is not as easy to see in practice. Words wound emotionally if not physically, and more importantly they can create a culture of resentment and anger that encourages and legitimizes hate crimes. Acts of hate are usually precipitated and accompanied by hate speech. For society to pretend otherwise—to ignore the causes behind ideologically motivated violence, to argue that speech and action can be neatly decoupled—is self-destructive. The framers of the Constitution protected speech because they believed the act of communication valuable to society in its own right.

What possible worth would have resulted from a Nazi march through Skokie, terrorizing the town's inhabitants and perhaps inciting people to dabble in pro-fascist ideas? The current First Amendment protection of hate speech, however well-meant in principle, hurts precisely those members of society least able to protect themselves—and, moreover, it is damaging to the principles of freedom and justice embodied in the U.S. Constitution.

The First Amendment does not forbid the control of hate speech.

Despite the Supreme Court's current protection of hate speech, alternative interpretations of the First Amendment have not been so indulgent. In 1942, the Supreme Court sustained the conviction of Walter Chaplinsky, a New Hampshire man who had caused a public disturbance in Rochester and spoken offensively to public officials. In his summary, Justice Frank Murphy spoke of a distinction between "worthwhile" and "worthless" speech. Worthwhile speech contained some social merit; worthless speech was merely obscene, slanderous, or needlessly provocative, and therefore not fit for constitutional protection. Justice Murphy went further and created a category of worthless speech called "fighting words," defined as speech that either "incite[s] an immediate breach of the peace" or—crucially— merely "inflict[s] injury" on the sensibilities of others. Although the term "hate speech" had yet to be coined, *Chaplinsky v. New Hampshire* effectively ruled that such hateful expression was not covered under the protections of the First Amendment.[5]

Later Supreme Court rulings overturned much of the *Chaplinsky* decision, including its worthwhile/worthless categories and its broad interpretation of fighting words. Nowadays the "inflict injury" clause has been dropped, and in order to meet the Court's definition, fighting words must be spoken in a face-to-face confrontation in which an immediate breach of the peace is likely. In fairness, many considered Justice Murphy's

FROM THE BENCH

Chaplinsky v. New Hampshire, 315 U.S. 568 (1942)

It is well understood that the right of free speech is not absolute at all times and under all circumstances. There are certain well-defined and narrowly limited classes of speech, the prevention and punishment of which has never been thought to raise any Constitutional problem.... The English language has a number of words and expressions which by general consent are "fighting words" when said without a disarming smile.... [S]uch words, as ordinary men know, are likely to cause a fight.

ruling vague, even at the time, and it probably needed refining by subsequent decisions. But for all its failings, it did point the way to another possible evolution of the First Amendment, one that protected genuine public discussion while excluding hateful or deliberately offensive speech. An absolutist stance on free expression is not an inherently more "authentic" reading of the First Amendment, one that automatically adheres to the intentions of the Founding Fathers; all the articles in the Bill of Rights are open to honest differences of interpretation. There is no necessary contradiction between respecting free expression and wishing to restrict hate speech.

The desecration of important symbols should not be protected.

Two of the most emotive examples of a deliberately provocative speech act in recent American history have been the intentional burning or desecration of the American flag as a form of public protest and the burning of crosses in a style made notorious by the "white supremacist" extremists of the Ku Klux Klan. Although the people conducting these acts are motivated by totally different ideas, the issues involved in flag and cross burning are really the same. Should actions intended to anger, offend, and in many cases intimidate be protected under the First Amendment simply because they are forms of political speech? There is a strong case against this.

The flag of the United States is the most revered symbol of the nation, one that the vast majority of its citizens hold very dear. Historically, the judiciary has not always been hostile to laws banning its deliberate damage. In a 1907 Supreme Court decision, Justice John Marshall Harlan wrote that "insults to a flag have been the cause of war, and indignities put upon it, in the presence of those who revere it, have often been resented and sometimes punished on the spot."[6] In 1989 and 1990, however, the Supreme Court specifically ruled that burning the flag was a form of constitutionally protected speech. Defenders of

A pro-flag burner lifts a burning American flag over his head during a rally held in Seattle, Washington, on June 13, 1990. The rally was organized by opponents of a federal law that would have banned the desecration of the flag.

the Court's latter decisions have argued that it is important to respect the rights of peaceful demonstrators even if they are behaving in a way that any given observer may find personally objectionable. If the United States begins to legislate which kinds of protest are tasteful and which are not, it will open the possibility of further restrictions on more important matters—the "slippery slope" argument. But is the slope particularly slippery in the case of flag burning? Does the act of desecrating a flag really communicate any serious political idea or viewpoint that could not be better expressed in a more acceptable manner? Is it really plausible that First Amendment rights will be placed in jeopardy if flag burning—an act that many citizens would consider repugnant and even hateful—is no longer tolerated by the community?

If anything, cross burning is an even more troubling issue than flag desecration because the intention is not merely to provoke or offend but to terrify people. Citizens across the southern United States are vividly aware of the symbolic menace of a burning cross, which racist groups have traditionally used to frighten people of different ethnicities and religions, particularly African Americans. In 2003, the Supreme Court found in *Virginia v. Black* that burning a cross could be criminalized only if done with the intent to intimidate. Because it might also carry a message "of shared ideology" among Klan members, burning

FROM THE BENCH

Texas v. Johnson, 491 U.S. 397 (1989) (Justice John Paul Stevens, dissenting)

The ideas of liberty and equality have been an irresistible force in motivating leaders like Patrick Henry, Susan B. Anthony, and Abraham Lincoln.... If those ideas are worth fighting for ... it cannot be true that the flag that uniquely symbolizes their power is not itself worthy of protection from unnecessary desecration.

a cross to express solidarity retained some protection under the First Amendment. In his dissent, Justice Clarence Thomas argued that the meaning of a burning cross was singular and mocked the idea of "an innocent cross-burner" who intimidates no one.[7] The meaning of a burning cross may be unmistakable to many, but the act remains protected under certain circumstances.

Hate speech can create a "culture of hatred."

Advocates of an absolute right to free speech argue that hate remains relatively harmless as long as it is not translated into action. This, however, ignores the insidious effects of such speech on society as a whole. When ideologically motivated anger is allowed free expression without hindrance from the law, what has been termed a "culture of hatred" can begin to permeate relationships among groups of people and, over time, begin to legitimize acts of violence—even including mass murder. Cultures of this kind have developed in recent years in places as far apart as Europe and Africa. In the former Yugoslavia, accusations against different ethnic groups encouraged the outbreak of a civil war that resulted in the deaths of thousands of Serbs, Croats, and Bosnians. In Rwanda, radio stations openly encouraged people to kill their neighbors, and the result was a genocide in 1994 involving up to one million victims. This is not to suggest, of course, that the United States faces the prospect of such a catastrophe. But there is a lot of evidence that hate speech, by dehumanizing its targets, can slowly remove social taboos against acts of violence and anger.

Summary

The defense of hate speech is ultimately a romantic attachment to a certain puritanical theory of society. It assumes that all public discussion has some kind of merit, that words have only rhetorical effect, and that deep down all people are open to rational argument. While one cannot doubt the sincerity behind these assumptions, they are not fully connected to the realities of modern American life. It is an unfortunate truth that a small but noisy and dangerous number of citizens are willing to abuse and exploit the freedoms granted to them by the Bill of Rights. These people wish to offend, anger, and scare others whom they dislike simply because of their racial or religious backgrounds or their sexual orientation. Hate speech is valueless and cannot be countered by force of logic, for it is beyond the reach of reason. If its practitioners choose to nurse their grievances in private, then the state should permit them to do so. But they have no inherent right to express bigotry in public. The ideas a country is willing to condone in the open forum say a lot about the kind of society it is and how well it protects its most vulnerable members. By prohibiting hate speech the United States would be extending, not limiting, its constitutional freedoms.

Banning Dangerous Speech Will Not Solve the Problem

In June 2008, the French film actress Brigitte Bardot was fined the equivalent of $23,000 for publishing an open letter to the French interior minister, criticizing the Islamic practice of ritual slaughter. This was not the first time that the famed movie star had courted controversy with her strong opinions about animal rights, opinions that have often spilled over into derogatory comments about France's large Arab population. In her letter, she wrote that Islam is "destroying our country by imposing its acts." In her 2003 book, *A Scream in the Silence*, which earned her a fine of $6,000 for inciting racial hatred, she protested the "Islamization" of France and voiced her opposition to "racial mixing."[1]

If Bardot had been an American, it is unlikely that any court would have been able to prosecute her for her controversial, but constitutionally protected, remarks. But France, unlike the

United States, has ruled that a citizen's right to free speech does not include the right to incite racial, ethnic, or religious hatred. To that end, anti-hate-speech legislation has been put in place to punish offenders like Bardot. The French are not alone in this. Many European countries have hate-speech restrictions embedded in their legal systems. In Germany, for example, it is illegal to display symbols associated with the former Nazi government of Adolf Hitler, such as the swastika. The emerging democracies in Central and Eastern Europe have either adopted such laws or are considering them.

What has been the practical effect of such legislation? On the whole, it has not been very successful. Extreme political groups have not seen any corresponding decline in their popularity. Indeed, the far-right National Front party, led by Jean-Marie Le Pen, won 12 percent of the national vote in the 2010 regional elections in France and drew as much as 22 percent of the vote in some areas of the country. Le Pen, whose commentary on the Holocaust had earned him convictions and fines in French and German courts, ran on an anti-immigration platform. Elsewhere in France, the president, Nicolas Sarkozy, headed a high-profile movement to ban the burqa, a traditional full-body garment worn by Muslim women. Decried as an affront to Muslim culture, the ban was defended as an appropriate rule in a secular European country. French law bans acts of hate speech against ethnic, religious, and sexual minorities, and the country is signatory to the pan-European "Convention on Cybercrime," which outlaws racist and xenophobic speech on the Internet. Despite these efforts, the increase in anti-Muslim sentiment and the growing popularity of far-right political groups in France are a troubling indicator that tensions between racial and ethnic groups in Europe may be on the rise.

What these examples show is that restrictions on speech, however well intentioned and crafted, are not the best way to tackle the underlying problem of political hatred. Not only is there little evidence that they suppress extremist ideas, but they can in fact fan the flames of hatred by giving extremists a mystique of martyrdom. The long-term consequences of hate-speech laws are usually ludicrous (as in the American "campus speech code" movement of the 1980s and 1990s) or sinister (as in South Africa during its apartheid era). To criticize hate-speech restrictions is not to downplay the genuine danger of extremism in modern American society, but the best way to neutralize these dangers is by using free speech against them, rather than trying to artificially narrow the range of debate.

A democracy must trust the judgment of its citizens.

Hate speech is one of the toughest challenges to a belief in the First Amendment right of free expression. Even the American Civil Liberties Union (ACLU), which has traditionally taken a very strong line in supporting controversial uses of free speech, has been divided by the merits of defending hate. As the ACLU leadership freely admits, the danger of allowing hateful words to go unchecked cannot be ignored. In fact, it is arguable that, if European society had taken more notice of the hate-filled rhetoric emerging from Germany and Italy during the 1930s, then many of the horrors of World War II might have been avoided. The temptation to restrict some of the ugliest expressions of hatred based on differences of race, religion, ethnicity, or sexuality sometimes feels overwhelming.

Yet such a rush to action—even with the best of objectives—is dangerous. Hate-speech laws turn out to be more damaging than the speech they oppose because they undermine confidence in the very principles of democratic debate, and hence democracy itself. Free-speech defenders are not naïve about the motivations of extremist political groups such as the Nazis who wanted to march in Skokie; they believe that these groups are not sincere in their pleas for "tolerance" and that to some extent they are exploiting the First Amendment. But however risky it is to romanticize free speech, it is even riskier to be cynical about it. The premise behind anti-hate-speech laws is too often that of the pessimist who does not really trust citizens to make sensible decisions of their own free will. Sadly, there are always going to be a few people in any society who choose to make bad decisions. But the historical experience of the United States shows that, on the whole, the public can be trusted as long as the marketplace of ideas is operating to distinguish good ideas from bad. Faith in the rationality and decency of the American people is implicit within the country's constitutional system, and to abandon this would be to chip away belief in the whole democratic apparatus.

Hate-speech legislation is a clumsy and dangerous tool.

The theory behind hate-speech laws is tenuous, but what about their practical application? Modern examples can mostly be found outside the United States, for it has become effectively impossible since key Supreme Court rulings like *Cohen v. California* (1971) to construct a hate-speech ordinance in the United States that will survive constitutional scrutiny.[2] The

FROM THE BENCH

Baumgartner v. United States, 322 U.S. 665 (1944)

U.S. courts have frequently ruled that freedom of speech includes the right to dangerous beliefs. In a 1944 case, *Baumgartner v. United States*, the Supreme Court ruled that a naturalized German-American man could not be stripped of his citizenship even though he had often made irresponsible remarks praising the Nazi regime. Justice Felix Frankfurter argued that foolish and immoderate speech has a place in a democratic culture:

> One of the prerogatives of American citizenship is the right to criticize public men and measures—and that means not only informed and responsible criticism but the freedom to speak foolishly and without moderation. Our trust in the good sense of the people on deliberate reflection goes deep.

results of the French attempt to limit hateful speech have been poor. Another conclusion one can draw from an international survey is that oppressive governments have quite often been the ones that have shown the most enthusiasm for hate-speech legislation. In the former Soviet Union, such laws were used to punish "defamatory" critics of the Communist Party regime. Turkish scholars investigating human rights abuses against the Kurdish minority have been prosecuted for supposedly spreading ethnic rancor. Perhaps the most extreme example was the Republic of South Africa during its apartheid era. During this period, which lasted from 1948 until 1994, the government banned all kinds of films and publications attacking its racial policies on the grounds that they incited hatred. Even the well-known TV movie adaptation of Alex Haley's book *Roots* was prohibited, because "a substantial number of blacks would . . . substantially experience great or greater hate against the white [race] as a result of seeing this film."[3] Clearly, these regimes were not interested in genuinely combating extremist ideas but in increasing their own control of public expression. Anti-hate-speech laws gave them a perfect tool to do this. Proponents of restrictions on hate speech complain that "hate mongers" exploit the First Amendment, often forgetting that anti-hate laws can much more easily be abused.

Speech codes are inherently counterproductive.

Perhaps the best example of the shortsightedness of attempts to limit offensive speech is provided by the curious rise and fall of the "campus speech code" campaign across U.S. universities and colleges during the late 1980s and early 1990s.

In 1986 and 1987, a number of racially charged incidents involving students stunned the higher education community across America. Offensive signs and messages were posted in public places or mailed to individuals. In one notorious case, a drunken campus brawl broke out between opposing white and black baseball fans. What made these cases especially troubling was that they frequently involved some of the best universities in the country, such as Stanford, Dartmouth, and Brown. If racist ideas infected even these elite institutions, then it seemed as if a plague of intolerance was affecting America's education system. In an attempt to combat this, schools began to create rules of acceptable student conduct that became known collectively as "campus speech codes." The codes differed from school to school, and some were more carefully prepared than others. Stanford's, on the one hand, was quite narrowly drawn up to punish only "fighting words" of the type ruled unprotected in the Supreme Court's 1942 *Chaplinsky* case. The University of Michigan's, on the other hand, was extremely broad, outlawing "any behavior, verbal or physical, that stigmatizes or victimizes an individual on the basis of race," as well as a host of other perceived wrongdoings.[4]

It was not long after the codes were introduced that their flaws started to become apparent. Lecturers complained that the codes had a "chilling effect" on classroom discussion because they discouraged students from raising controversial topics for fear that they might run afoul of a disciplinary charge. It seemed absurd that universities, which of all places in society should have encouraged critical inquiry and free debate, were now institutions with some of the least free speech in America. Oddly enough, at the University of Michigan, minority students ended up being charged far more often with code violations than whites. In 1989, a Michigan graduate student challenged the code in federal district court, and the judge speedily declared it unconstitutional, condemning its vagueness and noting that "the University had no idea what the limits of the policy were and was essentially making up the rules as it went along."[5] Other legal defeats followed, and the impetus of the campus speech-code movement sagged. In 1995, even Stanford's more limited code was overturned, despite the university's defense that Stanford was a private institution and hence not bound by First Amendment responsibilities. (This failed because California law explicitly bound private colleges to honor free-speech rights.) By the end of the 1990s, campus speech codes were effectively dead, and even though some colleges did not repeal their codes, they abandoned any attempt to enforce them.

Summary

"The road to hell is paved with good intentions," according to proverb. This neatly sums up the hate-speech law issue. There is no doubt that offensive, emotionally charged speech will always be a difficult test of the American commitment to free expression. The fear that hate speech can instill in communities is genuine, and it would be glib to simply state that words cannot hurt. But there is no contradiction between challenging anger while at the same time opposing heavy-handed censorship. A defense of speech is not necessarily a defense of action: Much violent conduct (such as the burning of crosses or the posting of offensive symbols on someone else's property) goes well beyond the constitutional understanding of "speech" and can be prosecuted on the more straightforward grounds of trespassing or criminal damage. Moreover, the First Amendment is the natural friend of all minorities or oppressed groups because it gives them the tools to take their case to the people. Rather than trying to suppress the superficial symptoms of hate that bubble up through speech, one should look for its more profound causes and neutralize them by positive and proactive measures—education being above all the best antidote to hatred. To genuinely fight hate one should use free speech, not limit it.

Obscene Expression Should Not Be Protected

In the fall of 1989, the chamber of the United States Senate was the unusual forum for a debate about the merits—or lack thereof—of some of the most provocative and controversial works of photography in cutting-edge American art. The storm centered in particular on the portfolios of two photographers: Robert Mapplethorpe, whose work involved explicit homoerotic images, and Andres Serrano, who had exhibited a number of pictures using religious icons in allegedly blasphemous ways. At the center of the debate was the Senator Jesse Helms of North Carolina, a Republican and a self-described conservative firebrand who had taken a strong line on issues concerning traditional morality and religious values throughout his career. Despite Helms's revulsion for the work of Mapplethorpe and Serrano, however, they were not the direct targets of his wrath. That role fell to the National Endowment for the Arts (NEA), a federal government agency created in 1965 to provide funding and support for institutional art centers such as museums and galleries, as well as individual artists. Throughout the 1980s, conservative watchdogs had become increasingly unhappy with the NEA's choices of supported art projects, believing that many of them were simply obscene or irreverent and skewed toward left-wing political ideas. Helms successfully proposed a new ruling that prevented the NEA from supporting any artwork judged indecent or which debased or defiled on the basis of race, religion, sex, nationality, etc. Grant recipients were also required to sign an oath promising not to produce obscene material.

The Senate rule provoked an equally strong counterreaction from the artistic community, which assailed these new restrictions as censorship and a violation of First Amendment rights. Censorship, or the deliberate government prohibition of speech, is a taboo word in the American system; it has always sparked angry resistance from those citizens who see it as

The NEA Saga—Censorship or Common Sense?

In the late 1980s and early 1990s, a number of conservative politicians, most notably Senator Jesse Helms, a North Carolina Republican, lambasted the National Endowment for the Arts (NEA) for its use of public funds to support artwork that many considered obscene. Critics called this an attempt at indirect censorship, but defenders said it was sound judgment. During a Senate debate on July 26, 1989, Helms himself argued:

> The so-called art community fails to understand—or deliberately refuses to understand—that a difference exists between an artist's right to free expression, and his right to have the Government, that is to say the taxpayers, pay him for his work. . . . I reiterate that there is a fundamental difference between government censorship, the preemption of publication or production, and government's refusal to pay for such publication and production.

inimical to the principles of the Constitution. Both the NEA obscenity clause and the oath were quickly challenged in court and thrown out.[1] In response, the Senate brought in a new provision dropping the oath and merely requiring the NEA to consider "decency" as a factor in making spending decisions. With the size of its overall budget under increasing pressure from congressional critics, the NEA strove to accommodate the Senate's demands, but in 1992, it found itself taken to court by a group of artists whose applications for funding had been allegedly overturned on the new decency standard. The case was settled in the artists' favor, the judge ruling that the "decency" requirement was too vague to be complied with.[2] It seemed by this that Helms's campaign against the NEA's policies had been thwarted, but instead the focus of his efforts shifted to simply cutting the agency's budget, which he accomplished with more success. By the approach of the new millennium, with the NEA a much-weakened institution, it seemed to many in the art world that the legal victories of the early 1990s had been temporary at best.

But did Helms's attack on the NEA really constitute censorship? Supporters of the obscenity and decency standards argued that it was nothing of the sort. After all, the Senate was not actually trying to ban the distribution or display of Mapplethorpe's or Serrano's photographs (though in an unrelated case, a Cincinnati arts center was unsuccessfully prosecuted in 1990 for holding a Mapplethorpe exhibition).[3] All Helms and his supporters were trying to do was to prevent federal money—taxpayers' money, ultimately—from being used to support such work, which a large proportion of the American public probably saw as lewd and without genuine artistic merit. Artists might have a right to create whatever they see fit. But does the state have an equal responsibility to support them financially no matter how shocking their work? To Helms and others, this seemed like an absurd abuse of the constitutional claim to free expression.

Obscenity is a valid category in American law.

The NEA affair underscores the continuing controversy over whether obscene speech ought to be protected under the First Amendment. Historically, the Supreme Court's rulings on obscenity have varied depending on the specifics of the case as well as the social and political climate of the times. The vagueness of some of the language does not help either: People commonly speak of "obscenity," "indecency," and "pornography" as though they were the same thing, but in legal terms they are very different. As of early 2011, the Supreme Court continues to uphold (with a few minor tweaks) a 1973 decision, *Miller v. California*, which says that obscene expression is unprotected by the First Amendment but that indecent expression—a less provocative form of speech—is protected.[4] So what is obscenity, as opposed to mere indecency? *Miller* defines it through a series of content tests that must be met. The traditional mixing-in of religious heresy—which the Supreme Court now explicitly upholds as protected speech—has in the past made the definition especially complicated.

Even though the precise definition of obscenity may remain a little blurred, there is enough general agreement—as Supreme Court Justice Potter Stewart famously remarked, "I know it when I see it"[5]—to make a category of unprotected speech possible and necessary. Not every form of literature or art that contains sexual content is without value to society, and indeed some challenging works—such as the novels of D.H. Lawrence or James Joyce—are now seen as groundbreaking. But other types of "speech" may well be prurient, offensive, or disgusting and have no genuine redeeming qualities. Not every explicit work is a *Lady Chatterley's Lover* or *Ulysses* awaiting discovery; more likely, it is simply crude. In an age of evolving technology, when it is becoming increasingly difficult for parents to monitor what their children are seeing on cable television or the Internet, it is all the more incumbent on society to protect minors from the worst of human nature.

Obscenity can be an issue of civil rights.

Traditionally, advocates of greater restrictions on obscene speech have made their case on the grounds of "community standards"—that is, they argued that, if the bulk of the population in a certain area considered a form of expression highly offensive, the local authorities should be permitted to restrict it. But this led to complaints about the "tyranny of the majority," since individuals had to submit to the tastes of their neighbors. During the early 1980s, a number of feminist lawyers and writers moved away from community standards and made the more innovative claim that sexually explicit material should be constitutionally unprotected because it violates the Fourteenth Amendment's provision that all citizens must receive equal protection of the laws. As previously noted, the First Amendment exists in parallel with a host of other civil rights, and despite its importance, it does not automatically trump the priorities of other constitutional guarantees. Some free-speech activists, such as Mary Ellen Gale, the former leader of the Southern California branch of the ACLU, were particularly keen to stress the importance of the Fourteenth Amendment in partnership with the First.

Two influential anti-pornography campaigners—Catherine MacKinnon, a law professor at the University of Michigan, and the late writer Andrea Dworkin—have suggested that, because of their demeaning and discriminatory effects on women, many writings and images that do not fall within the current *Miller* definition of obscenity are nonetheless forms of sexual discrimination. They argue that they ought to be unlawful because of the 1964 Civil Rights Act, which was based on the protections of the Fourteenth Amendment. Why, ask MacKinnon and Dworkin, are the rights of women to enjoy safety and freedom from discrimination under this amendment continually ignored in favor of the commercial-speech rights of people who produce pornography? MacKinnon and Dworkin contend that pornographic materials create an environment of hostility and hatred toward women and that the Supreme Court should be no more tolerant of obscenity than it is of racial or sexual discrimination in the workplace. This argument has yet to be accepted by the courts. It is, however, an important assertion of what has been called the missing language of responsibility in constitutional issues. Should not the state equally defend the wider community and the need of society as a whole to be free from offensive and demeaning imagery?

The Internet has made obscenity a bigger problem than ever.

Ever since the explosion in Internet use in the mid-1990s, the legal system has been trying to catch up with this enormously powerful and ever-changing medium of communication. One of the most pressing problems has been the supervision of children in cyberspace. The Internet provides unprecedented opportunities for young people to access information and ideas, but it also exposes them to new dangers. Not only is there a wealth of material inappropriate for the young available on the World Wide Web, but the anonymity afforded by the Internet has in some cases allowed "cyber-stalkers" to target, harass, and even instigate abuse of minors.

The government's attempts to regulate the Internet in the interests of protecting children have not been very successful so far. The most famous example was the 1996 Communications Decency Act (CDA), which forbade Internet users from displaying sexually explicit content online unless they had provided some kind of electronic filtering system that restricted access. A lobby including the ACLU, the American Library Association (ALA), and a number of professional media organizations vigorously opposed this act. These groups argued that filtering was better handled at the user's end by commercial software that blocked certain Web sites and newsgroups. But these user filters are not always effective, and parents—who often know less about digital media than their children—are technically unable to use them properly. The idea that there is a compelling issue of free expression at stake in allowing access to pornographic material is not very convincing. As Kristi Hamick of the Family Research Council said, "To pretend that our nation would somehow end if there weren't hard-core pornography within a child's reach is not only disingenuous, it's uncivilized."[6]

More recently, the focus has shifted to the role of public libraries. The 2000 Children's Internet Protection Act (CIPA) required that any library receiving federal funding must use an appropriate kind of blocking software to prevent minors from accessing obscene or pornographic content online. A lobby similar to the one that opposed the CDA in 1996 challenged CIPA, arguing that filtering software might block constitutionally protected speech. In 2003, the Supreme Court upheld the law. The court held that the purpose of the law was to allow libraries to function properly by prohibiting the accidental or intentional exposure of patrons to pornography. Because libraries have traditionally excluded pornography from their print collections, it would be appropriate for them to exclude online pornography as well. The justices noted that the law allowed librarians to disable the software to give an adult patron access to legitimate Internet materials. Any slight delay experienced by adults seeking "over-blocked" materials would be justified by the government's interest in shielding young library patrons from inappropriate content.[7]

One category of expression that American courts have consistently limited is child pornography, but not solely because of its content. Courts have punished purveyors to protect the children who are abused in the production of child pornography. Responding to the role of digital media in the creation and distribution of child pornography, Congress passed a law banning "virtual" or computer-generated porn that did not involve real children. In 2002, the Supreme Court struck down the Child Pornography Prevention Act as being overbroad. The court argued that some virtual child pornography might be considered obscene under *Miller*. Other material that does not exploit real children, such as pornography featuring adults posing as minors, however, might still warrant protection under the First Amendment. The court concerned itself with whether specific children were not harmed in the making of child pornography, not whether children in general might be harmed by sexualized depictions of "children."

Summary

Restrictions against obscenity in the United States have not always been fair. It is an unfortunate truth that a great deal of "expression" in twenty-first-century America is without any genuine usefulness to society. It may be big business—as the vast profits of the pornography industry demonstrate—but that does not make it widely acceptable. Whether obscenity is wrong because it offends local community standards, acts as a form of harassment against women, or threatens children, the government should have the power to regulate it appropriately. This does not—and in fact, should not—mean that all provocative or controversial art, literature, and speech should be prohibited. It does, however, mean that there should be a distinction maintained between forms of expression that genuinely contribute to society's sum of knowledge and material that is simply intended to exploit.

Government Should Not Decide What Is Obscene

In 1995, a Missouri computer repair technician named David Spohr, who had recently signed up with the America Online (AOL) Internet service, decided to use his Web space to create a fan site devoted to one of his favorite celebrities, the notorious stand-up comic Lenny Bruce. For five years the site existed peacefully, until August 2000, when Spohr suddenly received an e-mail from AOL notifying him that portions of his site contained "inappropriate" material and were being summarily deleted from the server. "I was shocked at first," Spohr said, "then somewhat amused and disturbed." After he complained to AOL, the company relented from its decision and allowed the offending portions of the Web site to be returned. As *USA Today* put it in an article about Bruce's latter-day brush with the authorities, "Thirty-four years after his death, the controversial comedian is still being hounded for his satirical stabs at government, religion, and American mores."[1]

It was a story that would have been wryly familiar to Bruce himself, who spent much of his career in the 1950s and 1960s fending off injunctions against his "obscene" comic skits. Bruce's act was not for the fainthearted; he took brutal aim at such sensitive targets as religion, politics, and sex, and he was not afraid to use language and imagery that many people found uncomfortable. Arrested six times from 1961 to 1964 on obscenity charges, Bruce was found not guilty by appeals courts in every case, but the strain of fending off multiple convictions took its toll on the comic, who died of a drug overdose in 1966. By the time of his death, however, Bruce had become a celebrated figure in the campaign to broaden First Amendment rights of free expression in America and he counted among his supporters such popular celebrities as the TV comedian and host Steve Allen.

In hindsight, what is surprising about the Lenny Bruce controversy is how tame so many of his "obscenities" now seem—the kind of language he was arrested for can commonly

QUOTABLE

Lenny Bruce

The raucous stand-up comedian Lenny Bruce was tried on obscenity charges several times in the 1960s. Despite Bruce's frequent use of foul and irreverent language, some critics considered his work an important form of social commentary. In his autobiography, Bruce cites a letter from a New York pastor in 1963; the text typifies a positive interpretation often applied to controversial artists:

> Clearly your intent is not to excite sexual feelings or to demean but to shock us awake to the realities of racial hatred and invested absurdities about sex and birth and death ... to move toward sanity and compassion. It is clear that you are intensely angry at our hypocrisies (yours as well as mine) and at the highly subsidized mealy-mouthism that passes as wisdom.

Source: Quoted in Lenny Bruce, *How to Talk Dirty and Influence People: An Autobiography*. New York: Simon and Schuster, 1992, p. 151.

be heard on such mainstream cable TV channels as HBO, for example. In fact, the closer one looks at Bruce's story, the clearer it becomes that his real crime, in the eyes of many public officials at the time, was not really obscenity but a kind of secular blasphemy—in other words, his disrespect toward the cherished political and social beliefs of the age. Bruce was performing during a period of great change in the United States, when traditional centers of authority like religion and government were under attack for their supposed hypocrisies and their possible complicity in injustices like the racial segregation of the southern United States. Bruce was doing something far more dangerous than uttering a few "bad words"—he was, through humor, making important points about the deep flaws in contemporary American society. The obscenity charges were just a convenient way of censoring Bruce's more important criticisms of racism, anti-Semitism, and other ugly realities. Despite his reputation in the 1960s as one of the country's most deviant heretics, Bruce considered himself to be a patriot. He believed passionately in the constitutional liberties of the Bill of Rights and felt that his opponents were the ones dishonoring American principles, not him.

Bruce's story demonstrates how accusations of obscenity are too often just an indirect way for people in power to silence those who have radical things to say about society. The continuing definition of obscenity as a form of unprotected speech by the Supreme Court is vague, arbitrary, and irrelevant to the genuine problems of, for example, keeping women and children safe from harassment or abuse. The law makes it clear that specific forms of exploitative material that almost nobody accepts as legitimate—pornography involving minors being one—are totally unprotected by the First Amendment and open to prosecution; such restrictions are entirely proper and would survive the end of obscenity as a legal category. But the current restrictions on certain types of sexually explicit speech are irrelevant to these real concerns.

Comedian Lenny Bruce flashes the peace sign as he steps from a plane in London in 1963. A few days before this photo was taken, Bruce had been barred from Britain "in the public interest."

The concept of obscenity is obsolete.

Throughout its history, the Supreme Court has often refined its definition of obscenity, but it has never really questioned why such a category of unprotected speech should exist in the first place. The Court has largely accepted it as an eternal truth, with little or no discussion. The explanation for this is largely historical. As part of its British heritage, the American legal system inherited the concept of religious heresy, sometimes called blasphemy or sacrilege, which included prohibitions on "bad" language but which was really focused more on questions of doctrine—the teachings of disfavored Christian sects and the denial of conventional religious practices altogether. During the twentieth century, as the United States developed an increasingly secular government system under the First Amendment's separation of church and state, these religious elements were slowly abandoned. In a 1952 decision, *Joseph Burstyn, Inc. v. Wilson*, the Supreme Court ruled that New York authorities could not ban an Italian movie, *The Miracle*, for being irreverent toward the Catholic Church.[2] In *Epperson v. Arkansas* (1968), the Court ruled that states could not prohibit the teaching of Darwinian evolution in schools on "sacrilegious" grounds.[3] As the religious core of blasphemy was stripped out, only the rules pertaining to indecent language and sexually explicit display—which were not the focus of heresy law anyway—remained. So in the twenty-first century, the United States is essentially stuck with the surviving remnants of an otherwise obsolete legal concept.

Some dissenting members of the Supreme Court that produced the *Miller v. California* definition of obscenity in 1973 (which survives largely intact today) made this argument nearly 40 years ago. Justice William Brennan, who had earlier been a supporter of decency laws, wrote that he had changed his mind about obscenity altogether. In his later life, he believed that it was virtually impossible to draw up a definition of obscenity that was clear and unambiguous, and thus all obscenity laws "failed to give fair notice" to the citizen—in other words, they were so hazy that a person could not be sure in advance whether he or she was committing a crime. Failure to give fair notice like this is considered to be inherently unjust in the Anglo-American philosophy of law. Brennan argued that, instead of the government acting as a morality censor, all adult citizens should be allowed to make private decisions about what was personally acceptable to them—although he still believed that the courts had a responsibility to intervene when children or unwilling persons were involved. Brennan and the other dissenters were outvoted, though, and *Miller v. California* became the standard.[4]

FROM THE BENCH

Miller v. California, 413 U.S. 15 (1973)

Not all of the Supreme Court justices were persuaded by the logic of the *Miller* ruling on obscenity. Justice William O. Douglas wrote an important dissenting opinion, denying the possibility of a coherent legal definition of obscenity:

> There are no constitutional guidelines for deciding what is and what is not "obscene." The Court is at large because we deal with tastes and standards of literature. What shocks me may be sustenance for my neighbor. What causes one person to boil up in rage over one pamphlet or movie may reflect only his neurosis, not shared by others. We deal here with a regime of censorship which, if adopted, should be done by constitutional amendment after full debate by the people.

Under the Miller standard, in order for speech to be declared legally obscene, it must be:

(a) whether "the average person, applying contemporary community standards," would find that the work, taken as a whole, appeals to the prurient interest;

(b) whether the work depicts or describes, in a patently offensive way, sexual conduct specifically defined by the applicable state law; and

(c) whether the work, taken as a whole, lacks serious literary, artistic, political, or scientific value). . . .

Obscenity law is frequently abused.

One of the most notorious abuses of obscenity law in American history, and an example that still carries lessons for the modern day, is the nineteenth-century "vice squads" of Anthony Comstock.

Comstock was a New England dry-goods clerk who moved to New York City in 1867. As an extreme Puritan fundamentalist, he was appalled by the "filth" that he encountered in the big city and was determined to end it. By enlisting the support of some powerful local industrialists, Comstock created the New York Society for the Suppression of Vice, which he used to track down and arrest alleged purveyors of vice within the city. In 1873, Comstock successfully lobbied Congress to pass a postal censorship law, known thereafter as the Comstock Act, which prohibited the distribution of "obscene" literature. Comstock's interpretation of obscenity was extremely broad. Works included under the Comstock ban included Voltaire's *Candide*, Walt Whitman's *Leaves of Grass*, and Daniel Defoe's *Moll Flanders*, and especially any material that dealt with contraception, or birth control. Comstock's influence at the height of his powers was such that he was essentially the sole arbiter of what could and could not be written in America, and his extreme religiosity became the benchmark for all definitions of "decency." He became a law unto himself and sometimes used his authority to carry out private grudges—he ensured, for example, that the works of the English playwright George Bernard Shaw were prohibited because Shaw had once insulted Comstock for his self-righteousness. The Comstock vice squads became a source of political power in the big cities of the Northeast and were used not merely to punish pornographers but also to legitimize the surveillance of citizens on political and religious grounds. It is worth noting that the Comstock Act remains part of U.S. law and was upheld as constitutional by the Supreme Court in 1957.[5]

The Internet should not be censored
on grounds of obscenity.

The high-tech world of cyberspace might seem a long way from Anthony Comstock's Victorian dry-goods store, but in the early 1990s, it seemed that the spirit of Comstock had returned to haunt the Internet. The innovative nature of this technology meant that an important question had to be answered before its free-speech status could be ascertained: Should the Internet be treated as a form of print material or as a form of broadcasting? This was important because First Amendment rights are not necessarily the same from medium to medium. Film and television companies are subject to much greater restrictions than newspaper editors over what they can depict to certain age groups—for example, through the Motion Picture Association of America (MPAA) ratings for movies. Although the interactive structure of the Internet is a lot closer to newspaper publication than to the one-way medium of television, computers bare a strong physical resemblance to TV sets. Internet advocates were worried that judges, who might not be very familiar with the technology of cyberspace, would presume from this vague similarity that graphics-heavy systems like the World Wide Web were indeed a form of television.

The U.S. government's first major attempt to regulate Internet traffic, the 1996 Telecommunications Act, assumed that the broadcasting model would be the standard for the future. Bundled into the Telecommunications Act was the notorious Communications Decency Act (CDA), which made it a criminal offense to disseminate materials that are "indecent" (but not technically obscene under the *Miller v. California* definition) to minors online without making a reasonable attempt to restrict minors' access. There was even a late-added amendment to the CDA that made the sending of abortion information on the Internet punishable by up to five years in jail or a fine of up to

$250,000—which even the Justice Department admitted from the outset would be unenforceable.[6]

Four months after the CDA became law, a three-judge federal panel in Philadelphia reviewed it and, in a 215-page report, threw out the new regulations entirely on the grounds that the Internet was clearly a medium closer to print than to broadcasting. "[T]he CDA would necessarily reduce the speech available for adults.... [T]his is a constitutionally intolerable result," wrote one of the judges.[7] The Supreme Court confirmed the Philadelphia decision the following year. The Internet was officially shown to be a medium with the same rights to First Amendment protection as books and newspapers. The anticensorship lobby had won—for the time being, at least.

Summary

In the United States, "indecency" is a protected form of speech and "obscenity" is not. But the justices of the Supreme Court have little clearer idea of the precise distinction between these

Communications Decency Act of 1996

(e) Whoever . . .

1. knowingly within the United States or in foreign communications with the United States by means of telecommunications device makes or makes available any indecent communication in any form including any comment, request, suggestion, proposal, [or] image to any person under 18 years of age regardless of whether the maker of such communication placed the call or initiated the communication; or

2. knowingly permits any telecommunications facility under such person's control to be used for an activity prohibited by paragraph (1) with the intent that it be used for such activity, shall be fined not more than $100,000 or imprisoned not more than two years or both.

two categories than any other group of American citizens. According to the 1973 *Miller* standard, obscene speech "lacks serious literary, artistic, political, or scientific value"[8]—often called the "SLAPS" test—but this is such a subjective judgment that it fails to give fair notice. It would, in fact, be vastly preferable for the United States to abandon the old religious-moral baggage of obscenity once and for all and to accept the principle that consenting adults should be trusted to make their own decisions about what they read or view. This would in no way interfere with society's need to prevent genuinely dangerous imagery—such as child pornography. But it would finally bring a close to the grim Comstock era and the exploitations of the law that were used against "heretics" like Lenny Bruce.

Freedom of the Press Should Be Restricted

In 1963, a group of relatively unskilled kidnappers led by a California businessman, Barry Keenan, abducted the 19-year-old son of legendary singer and actor Frank Sinatra from a hotel in Lake Tahoe and held him at gunpoint for several days until he was released unharmed. The criminals were quickly caught, and Keenan served a four-year prison sentence for his part in the bizarre affair. Thirty-five years later, Keenan, long freed from jail, was paid $450,000 by a Hollywood production company for the movie rights to his story. When Frank Sinatra Jr. heard about the latter-day windfall of his former kidnapper, he was angered at the thought that his frightening ordeal had made the felon wealthy and decided to have the payment challenged in California state court.[1]

He was able to do this because California, like many U.S. states, had passed a "Son of Sam" law in the early 1990s that required convicted criminals to hand over any profits they received from the retelling of their stories in book, TV, or film form as compensation to their victims. "Son of Sam" was a reference to the nickname of the notorious 1970s New York City serial killer David Berkowitz: The first Son of Sam law had been passed in New York after Berkowitz's conviction, because book publishers were allegedly offering a fortune for the rights to his autobiography. (Berkowitz never took advantage of any of these offers, so the law that bore his name never applied to him.) In 1991, the Supreme Court struck down the original law as an unconstitutional restriction on First Amendment rights,[2] but like other states, California had drafted its own version with that decision in mind, and its supporters believed that their more carefully worded law would be acceptable to the courts.

Unfortunately for Frank Sinatra Jr., this was not the case. Keenan's petition to the California Supreme Court in February 2002 was successful, as the justices unanimously rejected the state's Son of Sam law on free-speech grounds. Many traditional supporters of expanded First Amendment rights were pleased by the decision; others were less happy. Just as Senator Jesse Helms had argued that there was a difference between the government's censoring controversial art and its being obliged to finance it with public money, so critics of the California decision said that the right to tell a story did not automatically go hand-in-hand with the privilege of being rewarded for it. As the editorial board of the *San Diego Union-Tribune* wrote, "There's nothing stopping Keenan, or any other felon, from writing a book or screenplay or musical or whatever . . . but the Constitution does not say that convicted felons like Keenan have a 'right' to be paid for telling their crime stories."[3] Advocates for victims' rights saw the court's decision as a slap in the face to the victims of crimes, who appeared to be the biggest losers in a system that ensured that crime would indeed pay. Were, they asked, the rights at stake here really those of the media, whose only interest was to feed the public's insatiable appetite for lurid true-crime stories in a quest for profits?

The Son of Sam laws are named after David Berkowitz, seen here during an interview at Attica Prison in New York, on February 22, 1979. David Berkowitz, who became known as the Son of Sam after he killed six people and wounded seven others in New York City in 1976 and 1977, said the murder spree was due to an "unknown urge to kill."

This case is just one example of the way the much-hallowed freedom of the press is abused in the modern United States. The Founding Fathers rightly argued that newspaper editors need to be able to publish without fear of heavy-handed state censorship or the punishment of unpopular ideas. Such principles remain important today. But with rights come accompanying responsibilities, and sadly the experience of the past few decades has shown that the hugely powerful and influential U.S. media is often arrogant and exploitative in the use of its liberties. The law needs to be framed to guard genuinely important press freedoms but also to recognize that inadequate regulation of the media causes more harm than good and allows the rights of individual privacy and dignity to be trampled in a ceaseless, cynical rush for the public's right to know.

Prior restraint is not always unwarranted or unjust.

Prior restraint—sometimes also known as previous restraint—is an important philosophical concept in constitutional law that has special implications for freedom of the press. When the government enforces prior restraint, it bans the publication or broadcasting of something before it is distributed or sometimes before it is even written or made. This is in contrast to "ex post facto punishment," in which the authorities punish the authors for printing or producing something after it has been distributed.

Most people today would accept that prior restraint is a drastic form of government speech control that should not be lightly considered. Before rejecting it in too knee-jerk a fashion, however, it is important to consider some of the problems inherent in ex post facto punishment. Once something is published, the information has permanently entered the public record, even if the government later tries to suppress it. In short, if the speech in question was dangerous, then the damage has been done. The original issue at the heart of the 1931 case *Near v. Minnesota*, which prohibited prior restraint in the United States, is a case in point. J.M. Near was a scandal-sheet publisher who owned a virulently anti-Semitic newspaper, *The Saturday Press*, in which he made frequent scurrilous remarks about Minneapolis officials and alleged that a secret Jewish conspiracy was effectively running the city. In response, Minnesota officials banned further publication of the paper, which led to Near's appeal and the historic Supreme Court decision.

It is worth considering the special role of the press as a transmitter and magnifier of such offensive hate speech. If a single person makes a hate-filled comment aloud, the damage will inevitably be small no matter what he or she says. But if the same comment is made in a newspaper, it can have a much more virulent effect. Journalists are vastly more influential "speakers" in the marketplace of ideas than ordinary people, and their words carry particular weight, especially on the impressionable.

FROM THE BENCH

Near v. State of Minnesota Ex Rel. Olson, 283 U.S. 697 (1931)

Prior restraint of the press was explicitly declared unconstitutional in a 1931 case, *Near v. Minnesota*, which struck down a ban on an anti-Semitic newspaper, *The Saturday Press*. Not all the justices agreed, however, that the case involved a real breach of traditional liberties. Justice Pierce Butler was one of three members of the panel who dissented:

> [The stories in *The Saturday Press*] unquestionably constitute an abuse of the right of free press. The statute denounces the things done as a nuisance on the ground, as stated by the state Supreme Court, that they threaten morals, peace, and good order. There is no question of the power of the state to denounce such transgressions. . . . It is well known . . . that existing libel laws are inadequate effectively to suppress evils resulting from the kind of business and publications that are shown in this case.

Irresponsible papers like *The Saturday Press* do enormous harm by seeding lies throughout society, and even if ex post facto punishment is possible, the injury will often be irreparable.

It is not entirely clear whether the decision in *Near* is still relevant in today's online environment, where information moves with viral speed. Of particular concern are the rights of individuals whose private tragedy becomes public by way of the Internet. When California Highway Patrol officers leaked gruesome images of a young car crash victim in 2006, the victim's family hired a private firm to persuade thousands of Web sites to voluntarily remove the images. In a statement to the press, the operators of one Web site defended its refusal to take down the pictures: "Wanting to view photographs of tragic events is a part of human nature. . . . When we look upon photographs, like those of a young girl who has been violently struck down in the prime of her life by a moment's recklessness, we gaze upon our own mortality, and we think about how easily this could have been us."[4] Does the satisfaction of the public's natural tendency toward morbid curiosity justify the indignity of mass publication of a death scene? There is no doubt that the family involved—and many others—would welcome a ban on the publication of these particular photographs.

One area in which prior restraint of the press is provisionally accepted is the battlefield. As of early 2011, reporters embedded with U.S. troops serving in Afghanistan and Iraq are prohibited from photographing American soldiers killed in action. The rule is enforced out of respect for soldiers and their families, and photographers and reporters comply in exchange for the access that embedding with military units provides. As officials point out, journalists who do not accept the ban on photographing casualties are free to leave the protection of the military and cover the battlefield independently. While there is no general ban on the publication of images of dead soldiers in the United States, many journalists accept the burden of prior restraint to protect the dignity of the soldiers and to maintain their own access to the battlefield.

A press that is too free can
threaten national security.

The case for prior restraint is even greater when it concerns issues of state secrecy and national defense. The dilemma of how to balance respect for freedom of the press with the need to safeguard America's security was starkly highlighted in November 1979 by *The Progressive*'s "H-Bomb" issue.

Earlier that year, the magazine announced that it would soon publish an article giving a long and detailed description of how a hydrogen bomb worked. *The Progressive*'s editors argued that all of the information contained in the article was freely available in the public domain and that they were publishing it to increase awareness about nuclear disarmament issues. The government asked a federal judge to issue a restraining order preventing the issue of *The Progressive* in question from being published. Justice Robert Warren of U.S. District Court in Wisconsin agreed to this, saying that even if the article's information was theoretically from unrestricted sources, it was still a dangerous way of popularizing sensitive data. Would the article aid the nuclear programs of foreign governments unfriendly to the United States, even if slightly? If so, Judge Warren argued, it was better to use prior restraint than to take such a risk. The magazine appealed the restraining order, and the case was scheduled for review by the U.S. Court of Appeals for the Seventh Circuit, but shortly before the review was due to begin, the government, under increasing public criticism for its pursuit of *The Progressive*, dropped its case and the controversy became moot: The article was published that November. Because it never reached the Supreme Court, the case ended unsatisfactorily for everyone. The government lost its bid to have the article suppressed, but its right to issue prior restraint orders was not challenged in the courts either.

In hindsight, it is clear that *The Progressive*'s H-Bomb article was not a significant threat to U.S. national security. At the time, however, the case worried even some fellow journalists, who felt that *The Progressive*'s editors were being cavalier about genuine secrecy concerns in a bid to make an empty point about freedom of the press. Today, with the terrorist attacks of September 11, 2001, only too fresh in the national memory, the *Progressive* case has an even more troubling ring to it. In an age in which small terror groups can plot to build weapons of mass destruction, including chemical, biological, and even nuclear devices, can a nation afford to be puritanical about prior restraint when publications risk aiding its enemies?

Press rights can limit the rights of ordinary citizens.

The damage that the press can do to society is not always directly political. Indeed, it is sometimes caused by the media's obsession with the trivial in place of more substantial issues. The major media companies are often criticized as being part of a downward-spiraling race to produce the tackiest and least

FROM THE BENCH

United States v. Progressive, Inc., 467 F. Supp. 990 (1979)

In 1979, amid great controversy, *The Progressive* announced the planned publication of an article describing in detail the workings of the hydrogen bomb. Upholding a government request to ban the article's publication, the presiding judge for the U.S. District Court in the Western District of Wisconsin wrote:

> This Court can find no plausible reason why the public needs to know the technical details about hydrogen bomb construction to carry on an informed debate on this issue. . . . What is involved here is information dealing with the most destructive weapon in the history of mankind. . . . Faced with a stark choice between upholding the right to continued life and the right to freedom of the press, most jurists would have no difficulty in opting for the chance to continue to breathe.

informative books, TV shows, and films possible by appealing to the public's worst instincts and playing to "the lowest common denominator."

Crime reporting is a key example. The American press has a long-established right to witness and report on courtroom events. This was intended to make justice in the United States as transparent as possible and to prevent the imposition of secret and unfair trials, a laudable aim in itself. But this worthy goal has been distorted by the media circus that sensationalizes exciting courtroom stories without worrying about the possible effects on justice. Terrible crimes are turned into entertainment, and those involved in such cases are subject to merciless hounding by the media—which feels free to speculate endlessly on the possible truth behind the story, regardless of the traumatic emotional impact on the people caught up in the ordeal or on the jurors who are going to decide the outcome of a case.

No one who watched the Scott Peterson murder trial in 2004 can really deny that the intensive media interest had an influence on the events in the courtroom. Peterson, who was eventually convicted of murdering his wife and unborn child, was the topic of endless speculation before the trial and the subject of multiple books and made-for-TV movies afterward. Recruiting an unbiased jury became almost impossible because most potential jurors had already formed strong opinions based on news coverage of the murder. According to one of Scott Peterson's defense attorneys, the excessive pretrial publicity "effectively preordained a guilty verdict."[5] Attempts to counteract the effects of media intrusion, such as imposing gag orders on trial participants, seemed ineffective against the demands of 24-hour cable news. When a court trial becomes a media circus, faith in the fairness of our legal system is undermined. If this is the First Amendment at work, it is a curious form of "freedom" that so often puts the interests of media moguls above those of ordinary people.

Summary

During the first half of the twentieth century, the United States government began to regulate large industries in a previously unheard-of way, because it recognized that the state could not ignore their power to do great harm as well as good in society. The same sort of attitude is appropriate toward the industry that is the twenty-first-century American media, which undoubtedly performs many important and beneficial roles but is also capable of causing great mischief. First Amendment rights for the press are just as important now as they were when the Bill of Rights was adopted, but journalists cannot take cover behind the traditional dislike of prior restraint laws every time they behave irresponsibly toward vulnerable members of the community, national security, or the judicial system. It is essential that the United States temper its enthusiasm for freedom of expression in print and on screen with the acknowledgment that such liberties do not come without costs.

Freedom of the Press Is Vital to a Healthy Democracy

During the 1982–1983 academic year, a group of students enrolled in the Journalism II class at Hazelwood East High School near St. Louis, Missouri, published a short newspaper, *The Spectrum*, every few weeks as part of their curriculum assignments. When the final issue of the year was completed, the faculty adviser teaching the class left a copy of the galley proofs with the school principal for review, just as he had always done. The principal was not pleased by what he read. Two articles in *The Spectrum*'s special section on social issues discussed student pregnancy and the effects of parental divorce on children. The principal asked the faculty adviser to remove the articles, and the paper was published in an abridged version.

Some of the student journalists, who were not informed about the changes until the day of the issue's release, objected to what they saw as administrative censorship. After getting an unsatisfactory response to their concerns, they filed suit in federal district court, charging a violation of First Amendment press rights. This initial suit was unsuccessful, but on appeal the circuit court upheld the complaint. Hazelwood School District appealed in turn. In 1988, the case finally reached the Supreme Court. In *Hazelwood School District v. Kuhlmeier*, the Court ruled 5 to 3 that Hazelwood had not curtailed its students' civil rights because the First Amendment did not apply to them: The students were involved in an official school-sponsored activity (the newspaper had been published as part of a journalism class) and as such Hazelwood was entitled to exercise reasonable controls on what the students said or did as long as legitimate educational standards were at stake.[1]

Reaction to the Supreme Court's decision was swift. Civil libertarians complained that the Hazelwood ruling effectively stripped public school students of many of their rights of free expression and gave school authorities far too much discretion in what they could restrict in the name of educational necessity.

FROM THE BENCH

Hazelwood School District v. Kuhlmeier, 484 U.S. 260 (1988)

In *Hazelwood School District v. Kuhlmeier* (1988), the Supreme Court ruled that it was acceptable for public school authorities to exercise prior restraint on student-run newspapers. Still, some justices disagreed with the logic behind the decision. Justice William Brennan dissented:

> When the young men and women of Hazelwood East High School registered for Journalism II, they expected a civics lesson. . . . In my view the principal broke more than just a promise. He violated the First Amendment's prohibitions against censorship of any student expression that neither disrupts classwork nor invades the rights of others, and against any censorship that is not narrowly tailored to serve its purpose.

The case was cited in a number of lower court decisions in which schools were permitted to censor textbooks on grounds of "vulgarity" and punish student council nominees for comments made in their election campaigns. Legislators in California, Massachusetts, and several other states successfully introduced press protection bills that gave their public school students the rights that the Supreme Court had denied them.

The Hazelwood case illustrates several important, and often overlooked, truths about freedom of the press today. One is that constitutional decisions do not invariably go in favor of the media. Despite the widespread belief that American journalists have free rein to do virtually anything with the blessing of the courts, there have been a number of serious reversals for newspapers and broadcasters, with repercussions for the scope of free expression in the public forum. Another point about the Hazelwood case is that press freedom does not simply concern the mass media. Ordinary students in schools and colleges are just as affected by the Supreme Court's decisions as are CNN and the *New York Times*, and students need to be aware of the rights and restrictions that pertain to them too. The recent history of First Amendment press rights has not been a particularly happy one. In concentrating only on the media's occasional excesses and biases—and there is an unfortunate reality behind some of these criticisms—the public has tended to ignore the key role that a free press still plays in the democratic life of America. Zeal to condemn exploitative and salacious journalism must not destroy the liberties that have been so important in keeping the nation informed and alert to abuses of power.

Media scrutiny of the government should not be curtailed.

One of the greatest tests of the delicate balance between the freedom of the press and the need for state secrecy came with the Pentagon Papers case in 1971. This was the first time in U.S. history that the federal government had ever attempted to use a court injunction to exercise prior restraint on a publication: Its outcome was therefore of crucial importance for the future direction of First Amendment liberties.

The case began when military analyst Daniel Ellsberg allegedly gave a copy of a confidential government document that he had helped write to the *New York Times* and the *Washington Post*. The document, which became known as the Pentagon Papers, was a secret (and highly critical) history of America's diplomatic and military involvement in the Vietnam conflict, which was then at its height and the subject of great controversy in the United States. As soon as both newspapers began to publish copies of the Pentagon Papers in serialized form, the Justice Department petitioned federal district judges in New York and Washington to temporarily restrain any further extracts. The courts in each jurisdiction came up with contrary decisions, New York confirming the restraint and Washington refusing it, and so the Supreme Court immediately stepped in to resolve what was

The Pentagon Papers

The battle over the publication of leaked government documents by the *New York Times* and the *Washington Post* in 1971 was a critical moment in the relationship between the free press and the state. Author David Rudenstine summarized the Supreme Court's decision to overrule the government in his book on the case, *The Day the Presses Stopped: A History of the Pentagon Papers Case*:

> The Court decided to risk the dangers inherent in a free press because the alternative resolution—enhancing government power to censor the press—was even more threatening to a stable and vital democracy. This was a courageous decision supportive of the public's right to be informed about important public affairs.

Source: David Rudenstine, *The Day the Presses Stopped: A History of the Pentagon Papers Case*. Berkeley: University of California Press, 1996, p. 355.

clearly a major constitutional issue. Postponing its normal sum-
mer recess, the Court reviewed the conflicting decisions and in
a complicated 6-to-3 vote threw out the prior restraint requests
on the grounds that the government had not provided sufficient
evidence that national security was at stake.

Were the two Pentagon Papers decisions—*New York Times
Co. v. United States* (1971)[2] and *United States v. Washington Post
Co.* (1971)[3]—victories for the free press, then? In some ways, yes:
Publication of the serialized document continued, and the government was thwarted in its attempt to censor the two newspapers. On the other hand, the Supreme Court's rulings were very
unclear as to whether future prior restraint injunctions would be
constitutionally valid or not. Many legal observers felt that the
Court had missed a crucial opportunity to clarify once and for
all the status of journalistic freedom in sensitive matters of state.
However, the Pentagon Papers case had confirmed, at least to
some degree, the right of newspapers to conduct probing reports
free from state interference. The importance of this right became
even clearer just a couple of years later when two reporters from
the *Washington Post*, Bob Woodward and Carl Bernstein, inves-
tigated a series of wrongdoings involving high-level government
officials—the Watergate affair—that ultimately brought down
Richard Nixon's presidency. Without the guarantee of a free
press, Woodward and Bernstein's shocking revelations might
never have made it into the public sphere.

The press suffers too many restrictions in the courts.

One of the other tensions between journalism and the effective
workings of the state comes from newspaper and TV coverage
of courtroom cases. The Constitution guarantees all accused
citizens a fair trial, and some skeptics argue that this clashes with
the constitutional right to freedom of the press—and in some
cases ought to override it. But there is no necessary contradiction between these two rights; media coverage actually adds to

the likelihood of a fair trial. Unfortunately, not all judges agree with this, and an additional complication arises when journalists are privy to confidential information that might affect the outcome of a trial: Does their right to keep the identity of their sources secret outweigh the importance of courtroom justice?

The ability of judges to directly censor news reports of trials—often known as "gag orders"—was severely limited by a 1976 Supreme Court decision in which the Nebraska Press Association successfully appealed a prior restraint order issued by a state judge during a preliminary criminal hearing.[4] In that decision, the Court decreed that judges could authorize such gags on the media only if there was a compelling case that press coverage would make a fair trial impossible (for example, by prejudicing the potential jury pool against the defendant in advance). Since it is very difficult for judges to produce such overwhelming evidence in favor of a gag, they have largely abandoned attempts to directly limit press coverage. There is,

Gag Orders

In recent years, many courtroom journalists have been subject to legal obstacles, such as judicial "gag orders" forbidding certain people involved in criminal cases to speak publicly. The Reporters Committee for Freedom of the Press, an advocacy group for journalists, is concerned about this development:

> Courts routinely impose gag orders to limit public discussion about pending cases, presuming that there is no better way to ensure a fair trial. Many judges fear that having cameras in courtrooms will somehow interfere with the decorum and solemnity of judicial proceedings. Such steps ... may actually harm the integrity of a trial because court secrecy and limits on information are contrary to the fundamental constitutional guarantee of a public trial.

Source: Ashley Gauthier, "Secret Justice: Gag Orders," The Reporters Committee for Freedom of the Press. http://www.rcfp.org/secretjustice/gagorders/series.html.

however, a loophole in the 1976 decision: While judges may no longer gag reporters with ease, they can gag specific participants in the trial from speaking to the press—an indirect form of control that effectively prevents journalists from covering trials properly. Such redirected gag orders are increasingly common, and advocacy groups like The Reporters Committee for Freedom of the Press have complained that there is a creeping growth of prior restraint in America's courtrooms.

What happens when an investigative reporter who has gained important information about a criminal case from a confidential source is asked to name that source in the courtroom? If journalists reveal this information, they may be temporarily aiding the course of justice, but they will also be undermining the guarantee of confidentiality between the media and its sources, which in the long run could harm the press's ability to uncover public wrongdoing. And if journalists defy the judge's demand that they uncover source information in their testimony, they can be found in contempt of court and imprisoned. Former *New York Times* reporter Judith Miller spent 85 days in jail for refusing to name her source in a 2005 federal investigation of the leak of a CIA agent's identity. The Supreme Court had recognized a qualified privilege of source confidentiality in *Branzburg v. Hayes* (1972), but not when the information is of compelling relevance to the case and there are no other means of obtaining it.[5] Because the federal protection in *Branzburg* is rather weak, some states have passed "shield laws" that give journalists additional rights to keep their sources confidential. But the ever-present threat of imprisonment still acts as a serious restraint on many reporters working in America today.

The press is "a necessary irritant."

Because the public has grown increasingly disillusioned with the mass media in the past few decades, there have been suggestions that new ways should be found to "balance" allegedly biased press coverage. Some of the wilder excesses of intrusive and arrogant media coverage are to blame for this backlash, and it is unfortunate that newspapers and television have, to some extent, brought this resentment on themselves. The problem with legal corrections to the untrammeled freedom of the press, however, is that the cures are frequently worse than the original disease. In trying to suppress some of the more obnoxious tendencies of the media, the government may end up putting limits on the media's important constitutional role of informing the people.

Libel law involving public officials is a case in point. In March 1960, during the civil rights campaign in the segregated Southern states, the *New York Times* published an advertisement paid for by a campaigning civil rights group that made some comments about police behavior in Montgomery, Alabama. Although he was not specifically mentioned in the advertisement, L.B. Sullivan, a former commissioner of public affairs in Montgomery, objected to some factual errors about the police department he had helped supervise and sued the newspaper for defamation. An Alabama jury awarded Sullivan

The Danger of Public Cynicism About the Media

There has been a backlash of public mistrust against the mass media since the pioneering free-press cases of the 1970s, but as Bruce Sanford, an expert on privacy and libel law, argues in his book *Don't Shoot the Messenger*, too much cynicism may obscure the very important work that the media still does in protecting civil liberties:

> First Amendment freedoms should not depend so much on the public's approval of the press's work, or on the press performing public service, as on the recognition that as awful as they may behave at times, we are much better off relying on them than on government for our liberties.

Source: Bruce Sanford, *Don't Shoot the Messenger: How Our Growing Hatred of the Media Threatens Free Speech for Us All*. Lanham, Md.: Rowman & Littlefield Publishers, p. 194.

$500,000 in damages, a decision that the state's supreme court upheld. Although it was true that the *New York Times* had unwittingly published falsehoods about the Montgomery police, the Alabama decision was a serious threat because of the "chilling effect" it would have on subsequent press discussion of public issues. If government officials could sue newspapers for large sums of money whenever they made errors of fact, it would dissuade the media from tackling controversial issues at all. Fortunately, the Supreme Court overturned the decision in a 1964 ruling, *New York Times Co. v. Sullivan.*[6] The Court decreed that public officials could only sue the press for libel if there was "actual malice" involved in the misstatement—in other words, if the newspaper had known in advance that it was making errors of fact but had gone ahead regardless. The *Sullivan* ruling was a welcome protection against what could have become a major barrier to a free press.

Summary

The working of a free press has never been perfect. But if one wants to see an example of a "responsible," impeccably behaved media, one only needs to look at the trim and prudent output of the Soviet Union's official paper, *Pravda*, and the other newspaper organizations of Communist Eastern Europe in the 1970s and 1980s, forever pushing upbeat stories and never stepping out of line. However unpleasant the American media might sometimes be—and the nation should be constantly pushing for more substantive, mature journalism from American news publishers and broadcasters—it is still better to allow lapses of taste and good judgment if the alternative is the stifling of public debate. Attempts to bridle the press usually do more harm to democracy than good: For better or worse, journalists are among the most effective guardians in the defense of justice and truth.

The Current Challenges to Free Speech

The issues discussed here represent only a small fraction of the First Amendment controversies that are being debated in the United States today. Freedom of speech is a vast topic with almost limitless possibilities and points of honest disagreement, and it is unlikely that any common consensus about the "correct" interpretation of the right to free expression will come about soon.

Terrorism and Free Speech

For many, the most serious threat to American security in the early twenty-first century is international terrorism. The devastating attacks in New York and Washington, D.C., on September 11, 2001, made it clear how vulnerable the United States can be to aggression from extremist groups operating within and beyond American borders. They also emphasized the need for the government to act swiftly and effectively to protect citizens from other terrorist assaults. Part of the fallout from the 9/11 attacks has been an increasing tension between constitutional liberties on the one hand and the authorities' responsibility to investigate and prevent future incidents of terrorist activity on the other. Freedom of speech rights are considered among the casualties in this rush to preempt terrorism, as some people feel that their rights to patriotic expression have been curtailed in a corresponding overreaction against offending people of different races or nationalities.

In the decade since 9/11, groups like the National Coalition Against Censorship (NCAC) have catalogued a growing number of complaints about restrictions on free speech, either by government authorities or private organizations.[1] These range from the White House's request that the news media not carry videotaped messages allegedly recorded by Al Qaeda terrorists like Osama bin Laden to prohibitions on the wearing of American flag pins in college libraries for reasons of "sensitivity."

As evidence of new limits on expression, free-speech advocates point to the case of former University of Colorado professor Ward Churchill. In an essay published shortly after 9/11, Churchill displayed a callous attitude toward the victims of the attacks and expressed sympathy for what he imagined were the motives of the terrorists. In the wake of public outcry against Churchill's opinions, the University of Colorado Board of Regents brought his scholarly work under formal scrutiny. As a result of the investigation, his tenure was revoked, and he was fired from his professorship. After a protracted court battle between Churchill and the university, a jury confirmed in April 2009 that he was fired for voicing his (constitutionally protected) opinion. The judge, however, refused to reinstate Churchill in his position at the University of Colorado, and as of this writing, he continues to seek legal remedy. The heightened emotional atmosphere across the nation since the destruction of the World Trade Center towers and the attack on the Pentagon has, according

On April 2, 2009, Ward Churchill, a former University of Colorado professor, hugs a supporter after he was awarded $1 in damages from the school at his trial in Denver. Churchill, who had voiced sympathy for the 9/11 terrorists, was dismissed in July 2007 after the university concluded that he misrepresented or fabricated research on Native Americans and claimed the work of a Canadian environmental group as his own.

to NCAC, had a chilling effect on First Amendment liberties for both supporters and critics of the ongoing "War on Terror." Censorship of some kind is virtually inevitable during wartime, but what happens when the "war" has no clear boundaries or end date? If, as former White House spokesman Ari Fleischer

FROM THE BENCH

Whitney v. California, 274 U.S. 357 (1927)

Whitney v. California was one of several important cases to emerge from the "Red Scare"—the fear of Communism—that followed World War I. Anita Whitney was accused of collaborating with the Communist Labor Party in violation of a California law against "criminal syndicalism"—organizing support for groups that threaten violence or other illegal activities. In his concurring opinion, Justice Louis D. Brandeis discussed the requirements for state-imposed restrictions on political speech and free assembly. He argued that in order for state intervention to be justified, a danger to the government must be shown that is "clear," "imminent" or "present," and "serious"—that is, citizens or groups must be free to advocate, for example, the violent overthrow of the government, *unless* they evince a clear intention of when and how this is to be done and the effect of the planned action would be serious enough to warrant intervention. In the words of Justice Brandeis:

> Fear of serious injury cannot alone justify suppression of free speech and assembly. Men feared witches and burnt women. It is the function of speech to free men from the bondage of irrational fears. To justify suppression of free speech there must be reasonable ground to fear that serious evil will result if free speech is practiced. There must be reasonable ground to believe that the danger apprehended is imminent. There must be reasonable ground to believe that the evil to be prevented is a serious one....
>
> [E]ven advocacy of violation [of a law], however reprehensible morally, is not a justification for denying free speech where the advocacy falls short of incitement and there is nothing to indicate that the advocacy would be immediately acted on. The wide difference between advocacy and incitement, between preparation and attempt, between assembling and conspiracy, must be borne in mind....

has said, "There are reminders to all Americans that they need to watch what they say" in a time of crisis, will the hard-fought freedoms of the First Amendment survive intact?[2]

Free Speech and Mass Entertainment

Restrictions and First Amendment questions have always plagued the mass entertainment media, which tend to reflect the interests of the young, who in turn tend to rebel against the morals of the old. (Ed Sullivan thought Elvis Presley should not perform before a family audience, and the Beatles were denounced for their shaggy hair.) Of course, any speech act that seeks to entertain in a nontraditional way will draw criticism from those who hold traditional values. Hollywood has been regulated by the notoriously repressive Hays Code, the ineffectual Legion of Decency, and the imperfect Motion Picture Association of America (MPAA) rating system, but the mainstream now seems to have settled comfortably into the MPAA ratings. Banned books are no longer as much of an issue in education as they once were, and now an annual Banned Books Week, sponsored in part by the American Library Association, has become a celebration of intellectual freedom.

The largest issue now is that of labeling—the extension of the MPAA's successful rating system to other media. Since 2000, televisions have included blocking technology (the "V-chip") that allows parents to filter children's viewing based on the ratings encoded in television shows. While most viewers have noticed the ratings symbols on their screens, very few American parents use or even understand V-chip technology.[3] Still, Federal Communications Commission regulations remain in place, limiting what can be said or shown on television at given hours. A few well-publicized breaches of these rules (including singer Janet Jackson's "wardrobe malfunction" during the Super Bowl broadcast in 2004, which exposed her breast) have resulted in a more systematic use of broadcast delays of live events to avoid public censure and FCC fines.

In general, the trend in mass entertainment media has been to impose self-censorship to avoid regulation from the outside. A case in point is the video game industry's Entertainment Software Rating Board (ESRB), which assigns game ratings from C for "Early Childhood" to M for "Mature" and AO for "Adults Only." But doubts have often been raised about whether labeling protects children from inappropriate gaming material. Although most major retailers do not carry games rated AO, games rated M can be full of violence and sexuality. As long as there is labeling, there must be someone present to ensure that the labels lead to action. Because enforcement is left to the discretion of the retailer, the system has been criticized as comforting but ineffective.

Free Speech and Privacy in the Digital Age

Terrorism's effect on online speech—including the shutdown of Web sites with alleged terrorist links and the removal of information from government portals that could potentially be

FROM THE BENCH

Reno v. American Civil Liberties Union (ACLU), 521 U.S. 844 (1997)

In *Reno v. ACLU* (1997), the Supreme Court confirmed an earlier Pennsylvania court decision that the 1996 Communications Decency Act was unconstitutional. Justice John Paul Stevens wrote the majority opinion:

> The record demonstrates that the growth of the Internet has been and continues to be phenomenal. As a matter of constitutional tradition, in the absence of evidence to the contrary, we presume that governmental regulation of the content of speech is more likely to interfere with the free exchange of ideas than to encourage it. The interest in encouraging freedom of expression in a democratic society outweighs any theoretical but unproven benefit of censorship.

useful to terrorists—have been among the most visible signs of the post–9/11 atmosphere. But cyberspace raises peculiar First Amendment problems of its own, because its international character belies traditional state attempts to regulate speech. There is no tangible distinction between a purely "American," constitutionally protected Internet zone and the rest of the world. This means that individuals, companies, and organizations operating within cyberspace have little clear direction as to what free-expression rules apply to them, or what effect foreign government regulations may have on their speech.

One of the most striking examples of the clash between government prerogatives and free speech in cyberspace was the 2010 conviction of three Google executives for violating Italian privacy law. Since 1996, American law has protected Internet service providers (ISPs) from liability for materials published by users of their Web sites. European laws, however, have taken a different perspective. In 2006, a video of Italian schoolchildren abusing a disabled classmate was uploaded to Google Video. The video remained online for two months before the Italian police requested its removal. After it was taken down, the three executives were found guilty in an Italian court of publishing private information for profit. No one would argue that the video was a form of free expression by the accused, who had no knowledge of it prior to the trial. The executives, however, were held responsible for the company's practices and policies, which are legal in the United States but not in other countries. The Italian ruling is one of many controversies surrounding legal jurisdiction over speech in cyberspace.[4] Other issues include whether American journalists can be sued for online publications under other countries' stricter libel laws and whether American Web sites selling Nazi paraphernalia can be prosecuted under European antidefamation laws. It seems that, as cyberspace becomes an even more important forum for expression, there will have to be new legal paradigms transcending old notions of speech and nationality.

In the age of digital media, the boundaries between private and public life are more porous than ever. Twitter, Facebook, Second Life, and myriad other social media applications allow users to live virtual lives online, where thoughts, photographs, and videos can be published for all to see. Although the online world offers great freedom and flexibility, there is a dark side to having one's personal information constantly accessible. This is most vividly demonstrated when an individual's "personal" opinions and ideas negatively impact the people around them. Employers might use the Internet to evaluate job applicants as well as current employees. Unkind remarks, photographs, and revelations on social networking sites have resulted in school suspensions as well as libel or harassment suits. The consequences of cyber-harassment can be very serious.

The gray area between public criticism and private harassment is not peculiar to cyberspace. Beginning in 1991, during the Persian Gulf War, the U.S. military banned press videos and photographs of the ceremonial return of soldiers' coffins to American soil. The rationale was similar to the ban on photographing dead soldiers on the field of battle: respect for the privacy of the family. Since the entry of the United States into the war in Afghanistan in 2001, critics have argued that the consequences of war should not be hidden from the public, and the federal government lifted the ban in 2009. But the problem of privacy for the families of war dead persists. When a soldier dies in service to his or her country, some political and religious groups have aggressively argued that the soldier's death has public significance.

A radical religious sect based in Kansas, the Westboro Baptist Church, has repeatedly used military funerals as opportunities to protest the policies that, according to their beliefs, caused the soldiers' deaths. Their logic is convoluted: The sect's members claim that U.S. soldiers die because God hates American tolerance of homosexuals, Catholics, Jews, and seemingly just about everyone except the members of the Westboro Baptist Church.

The family of a soldier whose funeral was protested won their court case against the group, but an appeals court overturned the judgment. The Supreme Court heard arguments in the case in October 2010 and is expected to make its decision in 2011. At stake is the question of whether the emotional harm experienced by private citizens in particularly sensitive situations outweighs the right to voice constitutionally protected but highly unpopular and offensive opinions.

Commercial Speech

Americans have generally assumed that the focus of the First Amendment's protection of speech is on political expression. Nowhere in the language of the amendment is this specified, leaving open the question as to what other kinds of speech might be protected under the Constitution. The history of Supreme Court rulings over the last 100 years has shown an increasing willingness to count nonpolitical speech—speech with artistic, literary, scientific, or other merit, for example—as included within First Amendment rights. But the status of commercial speech, particularly that used for advertising purposes, is still unclear.

In the early decades of the twentieth century, Congress reacted to a host of complaints about dishonest and false advertising in the popular press by creating federal institutions like the Food and Drug Administration (FDA) and the Federal Trade Commission (FTC) to regulate the advertising world and to punish false and misleading commercial claims. The government's low estimation of First Amendment rights for businesses was apparently confirmed by a 1942 Supreme Court decision, *Valentine v. Chrestensen,* in which it ruled that purely commercial advertising was unprotected, and this decision held sway until the 1970s.[5] Then in *Bigelow v. Virginia* (1975), the Court made an important change in direction. The case involved an advertisement in a Charlottesville newspaper that provided information about legal New York abortion clinics. The managing editor of the paper was convicted of breaking a Virginia ordinance that forbade the dissemination of advertisements about abortion. The Court decreed for the first time that advertisements "of potential interest and value" to the general public were constitutionally protected, although the justices made it clear that false or deceptive advertising remained punishable.[6] Later Supreme Court decisions expanded this new ruling but still allowed federal authorities to limit false claims in consumer advertising.

In the digital age, the proliferation of unsolicited e-mail advertisements ("spam") has prompted efforts to regulate commercial speech in cyberspace. When some activists and Internet industries fought to outlaw spam, federal legislators responded with the Controlling the Assault of Non-Solicited Pornography and Marketing Act of 2003 (nicknamed CAN-SPAM).[7] The law provided some guidelines for regulation of unsolicited e-mail, and some spammers have been charged in its violation, but CAN-SPAM has not made a profound impact on the practice. Spam-catching software appears to have become the tool of choice for individuals and organizations seeking to reduce the burden of junk e-mail.

Campaign Finance Reform

Public cynicism about the effects of huge cash contributions on American political campaigns has fueled the drive toward new regulations and restrictions on the financing of elections. This move, however, cuts across the traditional interpretation of "money = speech" held by the Supreme Court, making attempts to ban types of campaign contributions an issue of free expression. The controversy has created strange alliances: The ACLU—which is in favor of public financing of campaigns but believes most of the recent legislation on the problem to be unconstitutional—has found itself in league with conservative lobbyists like the National Rifle Association (NRA) and the antiabortion National Right to Life Committee. What these unlikely political bedfellows share is a belief that too strict a form of campaign financing will inhibit their ability to speak out on issues of national importance.

The Supreme Court has not provided especially clear guidance. In *Buckley v. Valeo* (1976), it decided that contributions from individual donors to a campaign could be capped at a fixed dollar amount but that campaign expenditures as a whole could not be limited.[8] Twenty years later, in *Colorado Republican Federal Campaign Committee v. Federal Election Commission* (1996), the Court decreed that political parties and lobbyists could spend unlimited amounts on election campaigns as long as they did not directly coordinate their spending plans with the candidates themselves.[9] Finally, with the ruling in *Citizens United v. Federal Election Commission* (2010), the Court reversed a law limiting campaign advertising by corporations and unions.[10] With this 5-to-4 ruling, the Court established that expression by corporations deserved the same First Amendment protections as the speech of "natural" people.

All branches of government did not welcome the decision. The dissenting justices argued that corporations could not be granted the same liberties as citizens. President Barack Obama vowed to work with Congress to respond with legislation, or quite possibly a constitutional amendment, to limit the role of special-interest money in elections. The relationship between big-money politics and the First Amendment continues to change. What does the ruling in *Citizens United* suggest about the future of American free speech?

Summary

Freedom of speech continues to evolve as the means of communication evolve. There is a steady breakdown in the separation between authors and readers that is being accelerated by the growth of such media as the Internet. As self-publishing becomes an ever more common form of personal expression through the cheap and simple means of constructing Web sites, posting newsgroup messages, and sending e-mail, more and more people will be concerned with their rights not simply as members of a passive audience but also as active writers and contributors to public debate. Most of America is "the press" now, in one way or another, and First Amendment issues such as prior restraint—which at one time would not have figured very prominently in the lives of ordinary people—will become more and more significant to the mass of amateur journalists working in cyberspace.

Yet the long-term future of the First Amendment will also depend on the composition of the Supreme Court. Interpretive tastes change, partly depending on the general climate of the times but also on the political leanings of the justices appointed to the Court. The constitutional history of the twentieth century was one of the extension and entrenchment of the rights of ordinary citizens to speak in as many ways as possible; modern Americans have a much broader belief in the scope of the First Amendment now than their predecessors did a century ago. This tendency could continue, or the United States might just as easily see a contraction in the boundaries of free speech in the twenty-first century. The men and women appointed to the Supreme Court in the next few years may set the choice of direction. Judicial choices like these are not simply abstract news stories with no relevance to ordinary people. They affect every American citizen in ways that cannot easily be foreseen, perhaps, but which are no less important. This is why it remains important to be an active citizen, use the priceless resources bestowed by the First Amendment, and remain informed about changes in constitutional law. Speech will remain truly free only while there are people to listen, think, and respond.

Beginning Legal Research

The goals of each book in the Point/Counterpoint series are not only to give the reader a basic introduction to a controversial issue affecting society, but also to encourage the reader to explore the issue more fully. This Appendix is meant to serve as a guide to the reader in researching the current state of the law as well as exploring some of the public policy arguments as to why existing laws should be changed or new laws are needed.

Although some sources of law can be found primarily in law libraries, legal research has become much faster and more accessible with the advent of the Internet. This Appendix discusses some of the best starting points for free access to laws and court decisions, but surfing the Web will uncover endless additional sources of information. Before you can research the law, however, you must have a basic understanding of the American legal system.

The most important source of law in the United States is the Constitution. Originally enacted in 1787, the Constitution outlines the structure of our federal government, as well as setting limits on the types of laws that the federal government and state governments can enact. Through the centuries, a number of amendments have added to or changed the Constitution, most notably the first 10 amendments, which collectively are known as the "Bill of Rights" and which guarantee important civil liberties.

Reading the plain text of the Constitution provides little information. For example, the Constitution prohibits "unreasonable searches and seizures" by the police. To understand concepts in the Constitution, it is necessary to look to the decisions of the U.S. Supreme Court, which has the ultimate authority in interpreting the meaning of the Constitution. For example, the U.S. Supreme Court's 2001 decision in *Kyllo v. United States* held that scanning the outside of a person's house using a heat sensor to determine whether the person is growing marijuana is an unreasonable search—if it is done without first getting a search warrant from a judge. Each state also has its own constitution and a supreme court that is the ultimate authority on its meaning.

Also important are the written laws, or "statutes," passed by the U.S. Congress and the individual state legislatures. As with constitutional provisions, the U.S. Supreme Court and the state supreme courts are the ultimate authorities in interpreting the meaning of federal and state laws, respectively. However, the U.S. Supreme Court might find that a state law violates the U.S. Constitution, and a state supreme court might find that a state law violates either the state or U.S. Constitution.

Not every controversy reaches either the U.S. Supreme Court or the state supreme courts, however. Therefore, the decisions of other courts are also important. Trial courts hear evidence from both sides and make a decision, while appeals courts review the decisions made by trial courts. Sometimes rulings from appeals courts are appealed further to the U.S. Supreme Court or the state supreme courts.

Lawyers and courts refer to statutes and court decisions through a formal system of citations. Use of these citations reveals which court made the decision or which legislature passed the statute, and allows one to quickly locate the statute or court case online or in a law library. For example, the Supreme Court case *Brown v. Board of Education* has the legal citation 347 U.S. 483 (1954). At a law library, this 1954 decision can be found on page 483 of volume 347 of the U.S. Reports, which are the official collection of the Supreme Court's decisions. On the following page, you will find samples of all the major kinds of legal citation.

Finding sources of legal information on the Internet is relatively simple thanks to "portal" sites such as findlaw.com and lexisone.com, which allow the user to access a variety of constitutions, statutes, court opinions, law review articles, news articles, and other useful sources of information. For example, findlaw.com offers access to all Supreme Court decisions since 1893. Other useful sources of information include gpo.gov, which contains a complete copy of the U.S. Code, and thomas.loc.gov, which offers access to bills pending before Congress, as well as recently passed laws. Of course, the Internet changes every second of every day, so it is best to do some independent searching.

Of course, many people still do their research at law libraries, some of which are open to the public. For example, some state governments and universities offer the public access to their law collections. Law librarians can be of great assistance, as even experienced attorneys need help with legal research from time to time.

Common Citation Forms

Source of Law	Sample Citation	Notes
U.S. Supreme Court	*Employment Division v. Smith*, 485 U.S. 660 (1988)	The U.S. Reports is the official record of Supreme Court decisions. There is also an unofficial Supreme Court ("S. Ct.") reporter.
U.S. Court of Appeals	*United States v. Lambert*, 695 F.2d 536 (11th Cir.1983)	Appellate cases appear in the Federal Reporter, designated by "F." The 11th Circuit has jurisdiction in Alabama, Florida, and Georgia.
U.S. District Court	*Carillon Importers, Ltd. v. Frank Pesce Group, Inc.*, 913 F.Supp. 1559 (S.D.Fla.1996)	Federal trial-level decisions are reported in the Federal Supplement ("F. Supp."). Some states have multiple federal districts; this case originated in the Southern District of Florida.
U.S. Code	Thomas Jefferson Commemoration Commission Act, 36 U.S.C., §149 (2002)	Sometimes the popular names of legislation—names with which the public may be familiar—are included with the U.S. Code citation.
State Supreme Court	*Sterling v. Cupp*, 290 Ore. 611, 614, 625 P.2d 123, 126 (1981)	The Oregon Supreme Court decision is reported in both the state's reporter and the Pacific regional reporter.
State Statute	Pennsylvania Abortion Control Act of 1982, 18 Pa. Cons. Stat. 3203-3220 (1990)	States use many different citation formats for their statutes.

Cases and Statutes

Sedition Act of 1798

A very important early attempt to set limits on free speech; imposed fines and imprisonment for speech against the government. Heavily criticized but never actually ruled unconstitutional; it expired automatically after a few years and was never challenged in the Supreme Court.

Comstock Act (1873)

Criminalized the dissemination of "obscene" literature and information about contraception through the mail system. Courts permitted doctors to prescribe contraceptives in 1936, and the prohibition on birth control was removed entirely in 1971, though some portions of the act remain in effect.

Espionage Act (1917) and Sedition Act of 1918

The latter was in fact an amendment to the former; these were part of a major attempt by the government (under President Woodrow Wilson) to curtail free-speech rights during the hysteria surrounding World War I.

Schenck v. United States, 249 U.S. 47 (1919)

Established the "clear and present danger" standard for restrictions on speech content; source of the Holmes aphorism about shouting "fire" in a crowded theater.

Near v. Minnesota, 283 U.S. 697 (1931)

For the first time in American law, established that prior restraint is usually unconstitutional.

Chaplinsky v. State of New Hampshire, 315 U.S. 568 (1942)

Introduced the concept of "fighting words" to First Amendment issues.

New York Times Co. v. Sullivan, 376 U.S. 254 (1964)

Established protection from libel suits from public officials except when libel is knowingly and maliciously committed.

Brandenburg v. Ohio, 395 U.S. 444 (1969)

Established the "imminent lawless action" rule for restrictions on speech content.

Tinker v. Des Moines, 393 U.S. 503 (1969)

Confirmed public school students' right to political expression.

New York Times Co. v. United States, 403 U.S. 713 (1971)

Ruled (along with the similar *United States v. Washington Post Co.* case) that the injunction against publication of the Pentagon Papers was unlawful.

Cohen v. California, 403 U.S. 15 (1971)

Ruled that offensive speech (but not "fighting words") is constitutionally protected.

Branzburg v. Hayes, 408 U.S. 665 (1972)

Created a qualified right of confidentiality of sources for the media.

Miller v. California, 413 U.S. 15 (1973)

Established the foundations of modern obscenity law.

Nebraska Press Association v. Stuart, 427 U.S. 539 (1976)
Limited court-ordered "gag orders" on the press.

National Socialist Party v. Skokie, 432 U.S. 43 (1977)
Threw out bans on public marches by politically extreme groups.

Hazelwood School District v. Kuhlmeier, 484 U.S. 260 (1988)
Public schools can restrict the content of school newspapers if the restrictions are "reasonably related" to educational goals.

Texas v. Johnson, 491 U.S. 397 (1989)
Ruled (along with the similar case *United States v. Eichman*) that burning the American flag is constitutionally protected.

Simon & Schuster v. Crime Victims Board, 502 U.S. 105 (1991)
Threw out "Son of Sam" laws prohibiting former criminals from selling their stories to the press.

Communications Decency Act (CDA, 1996)
The two most controversial provisions of the CDA aimed to protect minors from harmful Internet content: They criminalized "knowing" transmission of anything "obscene or indecent" to anyone under 18 and anything "patently offensive as measured by contemporary community standards." Struck down by the Supreme Court in *Reno v. ACLU* in 1997.

Child Pornography Prevention Act of 1996 (CPPA)
Added "virtual" or "morphed child pornography" to definition of child pornography—images that appear to include children but in fact do not.

Reno, et al. v. American Civil Liberties Union, et al., 521 U.S. 844 (1997)
In a unanimous decision, ruled the two key provisions of the CDA unconstitutional for being too broad—not "narrowly tailored" enough to restrict only the kinds of speech they meant to restrict—and therefore violations of the First Amendment.

Children's Online Privacy Protection Act of 1998 (COPPA)
Prohibited commerce in the personal information of children (under 13 years of age) without "verifiable parental consent."

Child Online Protection Act (COPA or CDA 2, 1998)
Intended as a replacement of the thrown-out CDA provisions. Criminalized the commercial transmission of any material deemed "harmful to minors." Was struck down by *Ashcroft v. ACLU* in 2002.

Children's Internet Protection Act (CIPA, 2000)
Compelled public libraries and schools to install filtering software on their public-access computer terminals, with the intent of blocking the receipt by minors of inappropriate Internet content, in order to receive vital federal funding. Thrown out by the *ALA v. United States* ruling in May 2002.

American Library Association (ALA) v. United States, 539 U.S. 194 (2002)
Challenged CIPA; a federal court in May 2002 declared two sections of CIPA unconstitutional for requiring librarians to violate adult patrons' First

Amendment rights to free access of information. The Justice Department appealed the ruling to the Supreme Court—i.e., applied for certiorari—in September 2002.

Ashcroft v. Free Speech Coalition, 535 U.S. 234 (2002)

Declared CPPA unconstitutional because (1) it was overbroad, banning more images than it intended, and (2) such computer-generated images (or images involving adults pretending to be children) were not linked to the child abuse that motivated the legal objection to child pornography.

Ashcroft v. American Civil Liberties Union (ACLU), 535 U.S. 564 (2002)

The Child Online Protection Act (COPA) was declared unconstitutional by the U.S. Court of Appeals for the Third Circuit because its reliance on "contemporary community standards" made it too broad for a medium that distributed information on a national scale. The Supreme Court, which reviewed the case on the government's appeal of that decision, disagreed and sent *Ashcroft* back to the Third Circuit for consideration of First Amendment issues. Per order of the Court, COPA cannot be enforced at least until a final decision was made. On October 29, 2002, the Third Circuit heard the case again, and once again the injunction was upheld. On June 29, 2004, the Supreme Court found COPA unconstitutional.

Virginia v. Black, 538 U.S. 343 (2003)

Ruled that burning a cross could not, in itself, be criminalized. A state could criminalize only acts of cross burning that are undertaken with the intent to intimidate.

United States v. American Library Association, 359 U.S. 194 (2003)

Overturned *American Library Association v. United States* ruling (2002) and reinstated elements of CIPA. Established that requiring public libraries to install Internet filters did not violate adult patrons' rights to free access to information.

Citizens United v. Federal Election Commission, 558 U.S. 50 (2010)

Declared sections of the McCain-Feingold Bipartisan Campaign Finance Reform Act of 2002 unconstitutional for imposing limits on corporate spending on campaign advertising. However, the Court upheld portions of the law requiring that campaign advertisements disclose their sponsors' identities.

United States v. Stevens, 559 U.S. ___ (2010)

Overturned federal ban on depictions of cruelty to animals.

Terms and Concepts

Actual malice

Artistic merit

Brandenburg standard

Campus speech code movement

Chilling effect

Clear and present danger

Contemporary community standards
Content restrictions
Culture of hatred
Establishment Clause
Fair notice
Fighting words
Gag order
Hate crime
Hate speech
Imminent lawless action
Marketplace of ideas
Miller standard
Obscenity, indecency, and pornography
Political speech
Prior restraint
Protected speech
Prurient interest
Shield laws
SLAPS test
Speech act
Time, place, and manner restrictions
Tyranny of the majority
Worthwhile/worthless speech

Introduction: Free Speech and the First Amendment

1 Quoted in Martha Groves, Jill Leovy, and David Colker, "Student Web Sites Pose Rising Test of Free Speech Rights," *Los Angeles Times*, March 6, 2001.
2 Letter from Thomas Jefferson to James Madison, March 15, 1789.
3 *United States v. Stevens*, 559 U.S. ___ (2010)
4 *Schenck v. United States*, 249 U.S. 47 (1919).
5 Ibid.
6 *Brandenburg v. Ohio*, 395 U.S. 444 (1969).
7 *Near v. State of Minnesota Ex Rel. Olson*, 283 U.S. 697 (1931).

Point: Some Ideas Are Dangerous Enough to Merit Restriction

1 *National Socialist Party v. Skokie*, 432 U.S. 43 (1977).
2 *Smith v. Collin*, 439 U.S. 916 (1978).
3 Federal Bureau of Investigation. http://www.fbi.gov/ucr/hc2008/incidents.html.
4 Evelyn Beatrice Hall, *The Friends of Voltaire*, London: Smith, Elder, 1906. This quotation is often misattributed to Voltaire and is in fact modified from Hall. Hall claimed that she was paraphrasing Voltaire's *Traité sur la tolérance*, but she probably had in mind a sentence from Voltaire to a correspondent, here translated loosely: "I disagree profoundly with your ideas, but I would give my life for your right to express them." (Letter to M. le Riche, February 6, 1770).
5 *Chaplinsky v. State of New Hampshire*, 315 U.S. 568 (1942).
6 *Halter v. Nebraska*, 205 U.S. 34 (1907).
7 *Virginia v. Black*, 538 U.S. 343 (2003).

Counterpoint: Banning Dangerous Speech Will Not Solve the Problem

1 Henry Samuel, "Brigitte Bardot in Race Hate Row," *Telegraph* (U.K.), April 16, 2008.
2 *Cohen v. California*, 403 U.S. 15 (1971).
3 Andrew Irvine, "Free Speech, Democracy, and the Question of Political Influence" in W. Wesley Pue, ed., *Pepper in Our Eyes: The APEC Affair*. Vancouver:

University of British Columbia Press, 2000, pp. 29–40. http://www.bccla.org/othercontent/ 00freespeech.html.
4 "Speech Codes and Other Restrictions on the Content of Speech," Center for Campus Free Speech. http://www.campusspeech.org/speech_codes.
5 *Doe v. University of Michigan* (1989). Quoted at http://users.rcn.com/kyp/schools/bennet2.html.

Point: Obscene Expression Should Not Be Protected

1 Allan Parachini, "NEA's Obscenity Pledge Voided," *Los Angeles Times*, January 10, 1991.
2 Jacqueline Trescott, "NEA to Pay 4 Denied Arts Grants," *Washington Post*, June 5, 1993.
3 Isabel Wilkerson, "Cincinnati Jury Acquits Museum in Mapplethorpe Obscenity Case," *New York Times*, October 6, 1990.
4 *Miller v. California*, 413 U.S. 15 (1973).
5 *Jacobellis v. Ohio*, 378 U.S. 184 (1964).
6 John Schwartz, "Coalition to File Suit Over Internet Rules," *Washington Post*, February 26, 1996.
7 *United States v. American Library Association*, 359 U.S. 194 (2003).

Counterpoint: Government Should Not Decide What Is Obscene

1 "Lenny Bruce Still Testing the Limits," *USA Today*, November 2, 2000.
2 *Joseph Burstyn, Inc. v. Wilson*, 343 U.S. 495 (1952).
3 *Epperson v. Arkansas*, 393 U.S. 97 (1968).
4 *Miller v. California*, 413 U.S. 15 (1973).
5 *Roth v. United States*, 354 U.S. 476 (1957).
6 Reynolds Holding and Ramon G. McLeod, "Judge Limits New Law Curbing Internet Speech," *San Francisco Chronicle*, February 16, 1996.
7 "Hightlights from the District Court Ruling," http://www.freenewyork.net/quotes.html.
8 *Miller v. California*, 413 U.S. 15 (1973).

Point: Freedom of the Press Should Be Restricted

1 "Sinatra Jr. Tries to Stop Kidnappers' Film Rights," *Chicago Sun-Times*, August 14, 1998.

2 *Simon & Schuster v. Crime Victims Board*, 502 U.S. 105 (1991).

3 "Cash for Crime: Ex-con Challenges State's 'Son of Sam' Law," *San Diego Union-Tribune*, December 10, 2001.

4 Jim Avila, Teri Whitcraft, and Scott Michels, "A Family's Nightmare: Accident Photos of Their Beautiful Daughter Released," ABC News, November 16, 2007. http://abcnews.go.com/print?id=3872556.

5 Mark J. Geragos, "The Thirteenth Juror: Media Coverage of Supersized Trials," *Loyola of Los Angeles Law Review*. 39: 1167 (March 13, 2007): p. 1186.

Counterpoint: Freedom of the Press Is Vital to a Healthy Democracy

1 *Hazelwood School District v. Kuhlmeier*, 484 U.S. 260 (1988).

2 *New York Times Co. v. United States*, 403 U.S. 713 (1971).

3 *United States v. Washington Post Co.*, 403 U.S. 943 (1971).

4 *Nebraska Press Association v. Stuart*, 427 U.S. 539 (1976).

5 *Branzburg v. Hayes*, 408 U.S. 665 (1972).

6 *New York Times Co. v. Sullivan*, 376 U.S. 254 (1964).

Conclusion: The Current Challenges to Free Speech

1 Adam Liptak, "Before Justices, First Amendment and Aid to Terrorists," *New York Times*, February 23, 2010.

2 Richard Huff, "White House Sees Red Over Maher's Remarks," *Daily News* (New York), September 27, 2001.

3 Ronda M. Scantlin and Amy B. Jordan, "Families' Experiences With the V-Chip: An Exploratory Study," *Journal of Family Communication* 6 (2) (April 2006): pp. 139–159.

4 Adam Liptak, "When American and European Ideas of Privacy Collide," *New York Times*, February 26, 2010.

5 *Valentine v. Chrestensen*, 316 U.S. 52 (1942).

6 *Bigelow v. Virginia*, 421 U.S. 809 (1975).

7 15 U.S.C. 7701, et seq., Public Law No. 108–187.

8 *Buckley v. Valeo*, 424 U.S. 1 (1976).

9 *Colorado Republican Federal Campaign Committee, et al. v. Federal Election Commission*, 518 U.S. 604 (1996).

10 *Citizens United v. Federal Election Commission*, 558 U.S. 50 (2010).

RESOURCES ||||▷

Books

Amar, Vikram David, ed. *The First Amendment, Freedom of Speech: Its Constitutional History and the Contemporary Debate.* Amherst, N.Y.: Prometheus Books, 2009.

Bollinger, Lee. *Uninhibited, Robust, and Wide-Open: A Free Press for a New Century.* New York: Oxford University Press, 2010.

Currie, David. *The Constitution of the United States: A Primer for the People.* Chicago: University of Chicago Press, 2000.

Delgado, Richard, and Jean Stefancic. *Must We Defend Nazis? Hate Speech, Pornography, and the New First Amendment.* New York: New York University Press, 1997.

Foerstel, Herbert. *Free Expression and Censorship in America: An Encyclopedia.* Westport, Conn.: Greenwood Press, 1997.

Garry, Patrick M. *Rediscovering a Lost Freedom: The First Amendment Right to Censor Unwanted Speech.* New Brunswick, N.J.: Transaction Publishers, 2009.

Golding, Martin P. *Free Speech on Campus.* Lanham, Md.: Rowman & Littlefield Publishers, 2000.

Goldstein, Robert. *Flag Burning and Free Speech: The Case of Texas v. Johnson.* Lawrence: University Press of Kansas, 2000.

Hall, Kermit, ed. *By and for the People: Constitutional Rights in American History.* Wheeling, Ill.: Harlan Davidson, 1991.

Kennedy, Sheila Suess, ed. *Free Expression in America: A Documentary History.* Westport, Conn.: Greenwood Press, 1999.

Kolbert, Kathryn. *Censoring the Web: Leading Advocates Debate Today's Most Controversial Issues.* New York: The New Press, 2001.

Lederer, Laura, and Richard Delgado, eds. *The Price We Pay: The Price against Racist Speech, Hate Propaganda, and Pornography.* New York: Hill and Wang, 1994.

Lewis, Anthony. *Freedom for the Thought That We Hate: A Biography of the First Amendment.* New York: Basic Books, 2007.

Mackey, Thomas. *Pornography on Trial: A Handbook with Cases, Laws, and Documents.* Santa Barbara, Calif.: ABC-CLIO, 2002.

Nielsen, Laura Beth. *License to Harass: Law, Hierarchy, and Offensive Public Speech.* Princeton, N.J.: Princeton University Press, 2006.

Peck, Robert. *Libraries, the First Amendment, and Cyberspace: What You Need to Know.* Chicago: American Library Association, 2000.

Rudenstine, David. *The Day the Presses Stopped: A History of the Pentagon Papers Case.* Berkeley: University of California Press, 1996.

Sanford, Bruce. *Don't Shoot the Messenger: How Our Growing Hatred of the Media Threatens Free Speech for Us All.* Lanham, Md.: Rowman & Littlefield Publishers, 1999.

Shiell, Timothy C. *Campus Hate Speech on Trial.* Lawrence: University Press of Kansas, 2009.

Tedford, Thomas. *Freedom of Speech in the United States.* New York: McGraw Hill, 1993.

Walker, Samuel. *Hate Speech: The History of an American Controversy.* Lincoln: University of Nebraska Press, 1994.

Articles

Gilfoyle, Timothy. "The Moral Origins of Political Surveillance: The Preventive Society in New York City, 1867–1918." *American Quarterly* 38:4 (Autumn 1986): p. 637.

Web Sites

Accuracy in Media
http://www.aim.org

Electronic Frontier Foundation Blue Ribbon Project
http://w2.eff.org/br/

Fairness and Accuracy in Reporting
http://www.fair.org

The Reporters Committee for Freedom of the Press
http://www.rcfp.org

The four organizations listed above are some of a number that represent either journalists or readers and take strong positions on the issue of the freedom of the press.

American Civil Liberties Union

http://www.aclu.org

> The ACLU not only campaigns on free-speech issues but has also been a litigant in many key Supreme Court cases, such as the Skokie controversy.

American Family Association

http://www.afa.net

Eagle Forum

http://www.eagleforum.org

> The two organizations listed above believe in a more conservative approach toward freedom of speech.

Anti-Defamation League

http://www.adl.org

Gay and Lesbian Alliance Against Defamation

http://www.glaad.org

Southern Poverty Law Center

http://splcenter.org

> The three organizations listed above are among the principal monitors of extremist speech in the United States, and their extensive Web sites include a great deal of information about the problem.

Electronic Frontier Foundation

http://www.eff.org

> This site is a forum for discussing cyberspace censorship and contains news and updates on free-speech issues.

National Campaign for Freedom of Expression

http://www.thefirstamendment.org/ncfe1.htm

National Coalition Against Censorship

http://www.ncac.org

Office for Intellectual Freedom

http://www.ala.org/ala/aboutala/offices/oif/index.cfm

> The three organizations listed above represent a call for an extension of free-speech rights, and like the ACLU, are actively involved in First Amendment policy.

PICTURE CREDITS

ALAN ALLPORT was born in Whiston, England, and grew up in East Yorkshire. He holds a doctorate in history from the University of Pennsylvania. His book, *Demobbed: Coming Home After the Second World War,* was published in 2009. He currently teaches critical writing at Princeton University and is working on a social history of the British Army. He has lived in the Philadelphia area since 1994.

JENNIFER HORNER holds a Ph.D. in communication from the University of Pennsylvania. Her areas of expertise include American political history, the history of media and communication, and contemporary discourse in the public sphere. She lives in Philadelphia.

ALAN MARZILLI, M.A., J.D., lives in Birmingham, Ala., and is a program associate with Advocates for Human Potential, Inc., a research and consulting firm based in Sudbury, Mass., and Albany, N.Y. He primarily works on developing training and educational materials for agencies of the federal government on topics such as housing, mental health policy, employment, and transportation. He has spoken on mental health issues in 30 states, the District of Columbia, and Puerto Rico; his work has included training mental health administrators, nonprofit management and staff, and people with mental illnesses and their families on a wide variety of topics, including effective advocacy, community-based mental health services, and housing. He has written several handbooks and training curricula that are used nationally and as far away as the territory of Guam. He managed statewide and national mental health advocacy programs and worked for several public interest lobbying organizations while studying law at Georgetown University. He has written more than a dozen books, including numerous titles in the POINT/COUNTERPOINT series.